MY FIRST YEAR WITH IFS INFORMED THERAPY

A JOURNEY OF DISCOVERY, HEALING, AND DEVELOPMENT THROUGH INTERNAL FAMILY SYSTEMS THERAPY

MICHAEL LISTER
BOB KUCHTA

Copyright © 2024 by Michael Lister and Bob Kuchta

All rights reserved.

No part of this book may be reproduced in any form or by any electronic or mechanical means, including information storage and retrieval systems, without written permission from the author, except for the use of brief quotations in a book review.

Michael's dedication:

For Dr. Richard Schwartz

Thanks for listening so deeply to your clients and your Self.

Bob's dedication:

To Marshall. I carry you with me.

THANK YOU

From Michael:

Thank you to Bob Kuchta for being such a wise, compassionate, and insightful counselor, and then later for becoming such a dear, dear friend. So grateful our paths merged.

Thank you to Vanessa Serio for sharing so much of your pilgrimage with me over so many years, for introducing me to Bob, and for your help, support, and encouragement with this book.

Thank you to Jasmine Allen for your unconditional love, unwavering support, and endless, energetic encouragement. So grateful our 32-year journey led us back to each other.

From Bob:

I am thankful for everyone who has guided me to be able to contribute to the writing of this book: Mom for giving me the love of reading and writing, Dad for showing me how to let people know you care, Grandma Kuchta for her unconditional love, Liana for the space to be me, Rev. Jim for just being there, Marshall for the hope, Chris D for his kindness, Michelle G for helping me walk the path of IFS, and Michael for the opportunity.

I am grateful to Richard Schwartz for discovering this model and the many other teachers who have shared their wisdom.

Finally, I am thankful for Mandy for her steady presence and love; and for my kids, Jimmy and Mary. I love you.

INTRODUCTION

I entered Internal Family Systems Therapy in mid-life during a season of change and transition as part of an ongoing process of self development.

In many ways, I had been practicing self-therapy for a very long time, but I had only recently become aware of the IFS model.

For as long as I can remember, going as far back as early adolescence, a part of me always wanted to grow and evolve and become a better version of myself. And something deep inside me sensed that undergoing IFS counseling with the kind, knowledgeable, and compassionate counselor I had found was the next significant step in that process.

My season of change and transition had begun nearly four-and-a-half years earlier with the death of my closest friend, Dave Lloyd.

Dave and I shared a passion for spirituality, psychology, creativity, music, and helping others. Our connection was deep and profound, and led us to experience many of life's most sacred, significant, and meaningful moments together.

Dave's death and the void his absence created was followed

a few months later by a Cat 5 superstorm named Hurricane Michael that cut a cruel, merciless swath of destruction and decimation through the area I call home. Then, a little over a year later, long before our region had recovered, the entire world was devastated by a global pandemic.

This three-punch combination landed with incredible accuracy and brutal force. I absorbed the blows and continued moving forward, dancing, bobbing, weaving, undeterred, but it was early in the round and there were more barrages to come.

During this time of alienation and isolation, I lost most of what was left of my friend group—two to moves, one to a new job, one to marriage, another to divorce.

During this period, I also ended two relationships—one after nine years and another after only two—started a new one, sold my home of 25 years, moved 3 times in 6 months, experienced the generational shifts of aging parents dealing with illnesses, grown children navigating differing stages of life, and the arrival of grandchildren.

And all of this played out against the backdrop of the constant changes and ongoing ebb and flow involved in having a career as a novelist, inspirational writer and speaker, counselor, and life coach, and beginning a new journey as a singer-songwriter.

So much change.

So much transition.

So many opportunities for transformation.

Until I looked back at this season in my life while writing this I never realized the full extent to which my life had changed, never fully felt the tectonic shifts as they were occurring, never perceived the unparalleled upheaval I was undergoing. I never felt anything but love for my life, and apart from brief moments, continued to practice peace and joy and experience gratitude and equanimity.

In many ways, I felt unfazed and not particularly stressed—

even though I had experienced a minimum of 3 and quite possibly all 5 of the top 5 major stressors in life: 1) death of a loved one, 2) divorce or separation, 3) moving, 4) long-term illness, and 5) job loss.

My factory default settings are mostly positive and hopeful. For me, the glass is not just half but nearly always all the way full. In a room full of shit, I'm the little boy searching for the pony.

A few of my novels are in development for film and TV, which is a long, slow, arduous process. One of my closest friends asked me how I was feeling about the direction the *Double Exposure* film deal was taking—a process that has taken 12 years so far. I told him I felt hopeful and positive about it, but that, of course I would because those are my factory default settings. He said it's to my credit that though the universe has tried to beat that out of me from the beginning, I have held firm. He then added that many people had thrown in the towel long ago.

Not only did I arrive with these particular positive settings, but I was given a loving and secure foundation by my family, then spent my life building upon that foundation with spiritual practices and self-development.

This is in no way to say that I don't get down or experience existential despair or hopelessness, just that, relatively speaking, it's rare.

So if you had asked me at almost any point during this tumultuous time I would've said my life was fantastic. And it was. We had survived both the hurricane and the pandemic. It was a creative and prolific period for me. And one of intense spiritual and psychological growth. Ending the relationships I should've never started was, of course, painful, embarrassing, and shame-producing, but also liberating and exhilarating. I was experiencing the ongoing and indescribable joys of being a dad and a Grandude. Every change had brought with it endless and exciting opportunities. I was pursuing my passions, experiencing a rich and rewarding and fulfilling creative, intellectual, sexual, and spiritual life.

And yet...

I had experienced so much loss, upheaval, and change, I was living with an even more heightened sense of my mortality, and I was perceiving patterns, beliefs, and behaviors that weren't serving me well.

The patterns, beliefs, and behaviors I was most aware of, most focused on, were related to unrealistic expectations, an outward and other orientation, impatience, indulgence, a tendency for inaccurate, often romantic projections onto others, an imbalance between my head and heart, mind and body, moral perfectionism, an overemphasis on achievement, and an over-responsibility—that too often led me to attempt to assume responsibility for others.

It was here, in this moment in time and space, during this season of near constant change, tumultuous transition, and unprecedented upheaval, I entered my first year of IFS with a gifted and compassionate counselor, Bob Kuchta.

BOB'S NOTES

Nine years ago I was introduced to the IFS model. At the time I was preparing to attend a week long intensive training to learn EMDR (Eye Movement Desensitization and Reprocessing), one of the more effective models of helping people heal trauma. I had experienced the power of EMDR in therapy myself and was eager to share it. After the training it became the primary model I used in my practice.

Still curious about IFS, I decided to take a 6 month-long online course taught by the developer, Richard Schwartz, as well as two other senior trainers. As I learned more, I began integrating IFS into my practice, still primarily using EMDR as a foundation.

I love the work I do. I have always been curious about people. Now I have the privilege of hearing their stories.

To share some of my story, at 21 I experienced a life crisis after a relationship ended. I dove headfirst into the self-discovery and healing process and it became the focal point of my life for many years. My therapist and mentor, Dr. Marshall Jung, was a clinical social worker and professor. I decided to pursue a career as a social worker, working in the child welfare system in San Diego, CA for 15 years, initially as a case worker and later as a therapist. Between my personal experiences and working with traumatized children (and families), trauma became the lens through which I came to understand and process people's history, pain, and healing.

I have been married to my wife, Mandy, for 22 years. My son, Jimmy, is 14 and on the autism spectrum and my daughter, Mary, is 12. When Mandy was pregnant with Mary, we began making plans to move back to her hometown of Panama City, FL. It was 2012. I eventually started my own practice.

In 2020 I experienced another life crisis that led me back to therapy. I began working with a certified IFS therapist, starting a new chapter in my life. As I experienced the healing that the model and my therapist facilitated, it became my home base. I am so grateful.

I met Michael in early 2023. He was referred by a friend of his who I also work with. I knew of Michael and was excited about the opportunity to work with him. It has been a wonderful journey. You and I are fortunate that he has chosen to share it with us.

AUTHOR'S NOTE

From Michael:

This book contains nearly 40 of my fifty or so first IFS sessions. I have chosen not to include sessions in which Bob and I didn't do parts work, nor ones in which the parts work we did essentially repeated sessions already included here.

The format will mostly follow the pattern of Session, Insights, and Bob's Notes. I have written the Sessions and Insights, and, not surprisingly, Bob has written the aptly names Bob's Notes. Following a few certain sessions I've elected not to include an Insights section because I found I had nothing else to add to the session itself.

Throughout the book we have chosen to capitalize the names of parts and the Self.

Bob and I both sincerely hope that you gain much by taking this journey with us, and that it provides you with insight and inspiration for your own journey.

From Bob:

In this book, I share my experience with and understanding of IFS, but I am not a certified IFS therapist. I participated in a six month intensive online training led by Richard Schwartz, am very familiar with IFS literature, and for almost 5 years have been working with a certified and seasoned IFS therapist. I have integrated this into my practice and it has become a primary lens through which I work and support my clients. It has been life changing.

Michael and I want to emphasize that what is written in this book does not represent the opinion or official trainings of the IFS Institute. The IFS Institute has no responsibility for the information shared in this book.

In this book, "IFS informed" is intended to replace anywhere "IFS" is written. The use of the language and concepts of IFS is based on the authors' interpretation, and not necessarily that of the IFS Institute. The IFS Institute is not to be held liable for anything written in this book.

SESSION ONE

Preparing for my very first IFS session.

So excited.

Can't wait to get more help with the work I'm doing.

My Counselor is Bob Kuchta, a forty-something Licensed Clinical Social Worker from Big Bear, California, trained in, among other things IFS. He's open and gentle, wise and kind, intellectual and spiritual, and I can tell he's going to be a perfect fit for me.

Some things I want to address: caretaking, taking responsibility for others, being overly responsible in general, being more outwardly directed than I want to be, and any times I seek validation from and care too much what others think and feel.

I don't know a lot about IFS, but what I know really resonates with me.

Bob explained that IFS is a therapeutic model developed by Richard Schwartz that conceptualizes each of us as a system of interconnected, protective, and sometimes wounded inner parts, each with its own unique role and perspective, led by a core Self.

We each have a Self and multiple parts, or sub-personalities, and these parts can be in conflict with each other, leading to problematic behaviors and habits. IFS helps us identify and understand our parts and through the Self develop compassion and acceptance for all of them.

There are no bad parts. They may be misguided and misinformed, may go to unhealthy extremes, but they have no ill will or negative intent.

He drew a large "S" on a sheet of paper with smaller "P's" and "E's" in circles on it. The "S" is the Self, the "P's" are the Parts and the "E's" are the Exiles. The Self can be hidden and obscured by the Parts.

The self is the core of our being, the center. It is complete and compassionate, aware and loving.

As he was explaining this, I conceived of the Self as being, consciousness, essence, our original, authentic self, that divine center of our being that has been called soul, spirit, Christ nature, Buddha nature, and many other names.

He went on to describe Parts as the different aspects of our personality. They can be young or old, creative or destructive, protective, critical, joyful, and an infinity of other characteristics and traits. There are no bad parts, and every part has a job.

Parts can have burdens, which are the beliefs about and the emotional pain and suffering that we carry from past experiences.

Exiles are the parts of us that we have been banished for their protection, and they often carry our deepest wounds and greatest shame.

Unblending is the process of becoming aware of our different parts and their entanglements and learning to see them more clearly.

Self-therapy or self-leadership is the ability to lead our lives from a place of Self, from our core, our center, from our divine nature. It means being able to make choices that are aligned with our values, even when our parts are trying to lead us in a different direction. It is also working with our parts who, now with Self-led leadership and self-therapy, can take on more healthy and beneficial roles or approaches to their roles, once the shame and pain they were protecting us from has been released.

The Four Goals of IFS are: to liberate parts from the roles they've been forced into so they can be who they were meant to be, to restore trust in the Self and Self-leadership, re-harmonize the inner system, to become Self-led in our interactions with the world.

The Eight C's of self: 1) calmness, 2) curiosity, 3) compassion, 4) confidence, 5) courage, 6) creativity, 7) clarity, 8) connectedness.

The Five Characteristics about Parts: 1) parts are innate, 2) there are no bad parts, 3) you often have to earn the trust of your parts, 4) they can cause a lot of damage, 5) they are very important and deserve serious attention and consideration.

INSIGHTS

Things I jotted down in the session: The mosaic mind. "Inside out." All parts have a purpose. Protectors say "Never again." Firefighters try to numb. Exiles are who Protectors and Firefighters are protecting. The goal is softening, unblending, and unburdening.

List of possible parts: dad, novelist, creator, healer, the teacher, the counselor, the musician, caretaker, seeker, perfectionist, schemer, romantic, playful, prankster, the pusher, impatient, driven, the PR manager, the figure-outer, the suppressor, the promoter, the embarrassed, the appreciator, the connector, the people pleaser, the peacekeeper, the shamed, the little boy, the teenager, the fixer.

My word for this year is Awareness.

And on the morning I chose that as my word or it chose me, the meditation that first popped up under "For You" on my meditation app was "Cultivating Awareness."

I'm so grateful for the sell of my home and the opportunities that affords me.

I'm excited about the present and the future.

I'm so pleased, grateful, and excited about working with Bob in IFS.

I love my life.

I love my Self.

After I played pickup basketball at the old gym last night, my granddaughter and I played on the dirt pile on the side of the gym. She is so much fun! She plays and pretends so well. I love playing with her. Enjoy how magic it is. I love to play and pretend, to create, to dance, to sing, and to play ball. What a gift playing is!

I want to be free. Truly free. Free to play even more than I already do.

I want to let go of and be unburdened by anything that blocks my flow—the flow that allows me to play and love with abandon.

Everything is a process. I'm in process.

BOB'S NOTES

When I graduated from high school, I wanted to be a teacher. Outside of my parents, they'd had the biggest impact on my life. Many of them stoked my curiosity and a love of learning.

Teaching is one of my favorite parts of being a therapist. The key is knowing when to teach and when to listen.

In the online trainings by Richard Schwartz, he uses the acronym WAIT for "Why Am I Talking." As a therapist what I know or say doesn't matter if I don't have my client's trust. Therapy begins in the relationship. Creating a safe, nurturing environment comes first. Carl Rogers referred to it as "unconditional positive regard." Trust is the foundation of attachment

So I let the client lead. Some folks need a few sessions to tell their story and feel me out before they begin testing the waters. Some, like Michael, are ready from the get go.

SESSION TWO

A small-town little league field beneath a looming late afternoon Florida sun.

An itchy, ill-fitting red and white baseball uniform branded with the name of the local grocery store on the skinny body of a seven-year-old little boy with prominent front teeth.

Heart rate elevated, trickles of sweat snaking down his back even before the start of the game.

Nervous stomach requires him to sprint across the side street to use the restroom in the small, old community building.

My first session involving parts work begins with a body scan.

As I sit there, eyes closed, calmly breathing, I became aware of my body.

Surveying my body, I find tension, nervousness, and anxiety in my lower abdomen.

The activated part that appears is a seven-year-old little league baseball player, who is nervous before his game. The pitcher for the opposing team, whose nickname is Ox, is an oversized boy in a man's body with a wild, violent fastball that often strikes the opposing team's players at bat.

My little seven-year-old part wants to perform well, not get embarrassed, not get hit.

He's a gentle, sensitive, somewhat shy boy with a desire to do well and garner the approval of adults and to a lesser extent peers.

I am moved with care and compassion for him, and a part of me wants to comfort and reassure him, and let him know he's seen and safe and cared for, and doesn't need to be involved in little league or anything else he doesn't want to.

He places a good bit of pressure on himself—a pressure that does not come, outwardly at least, from his parents or his coach, but is innate, internalized, encouraged by certain peers and their parents and some of the other coaches.

He doesn't really enjoy playing baseball, but it never occurs to him to stop until a few years later, at which point he refuses to give into peer, coach, and community pressure to play football and baseball in school, following instead his love of basketball and joining a far more marginalized part of the student body.

Bob asks who that little boy thinks I am.

When I inquire, it's clear he thinks I'm him—still that sweet, shy little baseball player.

Bob encourages me to show him who I really am now.

I do.

The little boy part is shocked.

He sees me as a man in middle-age—older than all the coaches and parents involved in little league back then.

The little boy sees that I am grown, strong, secure, calm, confident, and that I don't give into peer pressure or spend time doing an activity like baseball that I don't want to do.

He experiences a rush of freedom and sense of safety and loses all his nervousness and fear and desire to please.

Above all else, he sees I'm a safe place.

Bob asks me to ask him what he wants.

He tells me he'd like to get away.

I take him to the now dim and empty ball field and we sit together in the empty metal bleachers near the old green cinderblock dugout.

His experience now is completely different than when he was here as a kid.

He feels safe and calm, comfortable and at ease.

He trusts me completely, knows I'm a good dad and can handle anything that comes up. It is a powerful and profound experience.

I cry cathartically throughout the session and experience a release and freedom, as does my seven-year-old little league baseball player part.

INSIGHTS

Prior to this session, I wondered how I would respond to IFS parts work.

Would any parts come forward? What would I do if they didn't?

I'm a creative, a novelist and storyteller. I have an active and vivid imagination. Would part of me be tempted to create a part or story to fill the void if nothing happened?

I didn't know a lot about IFS, but I was concerned that I had read and heard enough that there might be a part of me that would make something up instead of allowing for a more authentic unfolding.

As it happened, I slipped comfortably and immediately into parts work and found it to be a profound and cathartic experience, which I'm sure has a lot to do with what an excellent counselor Bob is.

I've spent decades in self-development, spiritual and psychological practices, and I feel like everything I've done has prepared me for this, for IFS work with Bob. I know there are many good and effective and tested counseling techniques out there, but as much as I've studied and practiced and benefited from them, none have resonated with me as much, nor seemed as complete and accurate to the human experience as IFS.

The IFS model and my experience of it reminds me of the poem, The Guest House, by the 13th Century Persian Sufi mystic Jalal al-Din Rumi.

This being human is a guest house.
    Every morning a new arrival.

A joy, a depression, a meanness,
    some momentary awareness comes
    As an unexpected visitor.

Welcome and entertain them all!
    Even if they're a crowd of sorrows,
    who violently sweep your house
    empty of its furniture,
    still treat each guest honorably.
    He may be clearing you out
    for some new delight.

The dark thought, the shame, the malice,
    meet them at the door laughing,
    and invite them in.

Be grateful for whoever comes,
    because each has been sent
    as a guide from beyond.

To me, Rumi's "unexpected visitors" are our parts. They are already in our house. Their "arrival" happens when they are activated. And our job is to welcome them with open, calm, compassionate curiosity.

BOB'S NOTES

Most therapeutic modalities use a "top down" approach. That means starting with the "head" (or "mind") focusing on what we know, observe, believe, etc. It has value, but it is only a part of the equation. "Bottom up", or a body/somatic based approach has equal value. In my experience they complement each other. Yin and Yang. "Top down" had been my primary orientation until I was well into my experience receiving IFS.

Most of us enter therapy in a state of crisis. "Going inside" ourselves, so to speak, isn't safe. We are hesitant to go inside our own minds, let alone our bodies. Unlike many of us, Michael entered therapy from a safe, curious place.

Trust must be developed with our therapist and then within ourselves. I have been reminded that the role of the therapist in IFS is to hold what we call "Self Energy." My mentor. Marshall Jung, might call it "Hope."

SESSION THREE

Evening in the French Quarter, the setting sun diffusing cobblestone streets, verdant ferns hanging from the wrought iron railings of balconies, walled courtyards, and the colorful Creole cottages with a warm orange-gold glow.

I duck into a small cigar shop on Orleans Avenue.

As I'm looking around, the middle-age woman working the shop approaches me.

She's a seer and wants to tell me what she sees.

As we talk, or rather as she talks and I listen, attempting to understand what she is saying, she begins to write words and numbers and symbols on the inside flap of a disassembled cigarette carton.

Much of what she says is lost in translation, but the three main takeaways are my number is one, I need to write more and talk less, and I have a big, big heart. This last she repeats many times during the twenty-minutes or so she tells me what she is seeing and hearing about me. *You have a big, big heart. A big, big heart.*

I am reminded of this experience during the parts work I do in my session this week.

As I scan my body, I become aware of a soft, warm orange glow next to my heart, an amber aura.

Amber is the color of your energy echoes through me as the song plays on my internal sound system.

This part has presence more than persona, energy more than personality. I perceive it as a force, an angel, a messenger.

In some ways this part is there to protect my heart. In other ways it seems like it's emanating from my heart.

When the part says it's there to protect my heart, another part says my heart doesn't need protecting, that it is big and strong and powerful.

In addition to being a protector and messenger, the part says it's a witnesses.

I begin to cry.

I recall the cigar shop lady in the Quarter.

Her words reverberate through me. *You have a big, big heart. Such a big, big heart.*

I cry a lot more.

Walking into a cigar shop in the Quarter and having a stranger see something in me and hear a message for me made me feel seen and loved and cared for.

It has happened a number of times during my life—someone, often a stranger, serving as an angel, a messenger for me, giving me a word from the beyond.

The part says that my huge heart needs protecting, caring for, and that's its job.

I had cried a good bit in my previous session, but cry far more during this one.

I feel seen and loved and cared for all over again.

The person who walked with me into that fateful cigar shop was skeptical and cynical of the entire experience, and seemed impatient, irritated, and even jealous. That same person frequently expressed those same sentiments and far, far worse, often spewing hateful and outlandish accusations that could certainly be characterized as attacks of, among other things, my heart.

And in eight months from that moment in that cigar shop that person was no longer in my life.

Not for the first time in my life I felt protected, loved, and cared for. And in such a way that it was obvious what was happening and only required me to lovingly let it happen.

I cried tears of love and gratitude, of healing and joy, and felt the sweetest release.

Then, for the first of many times, my Seeker Part comes forward.

He seeks for knowledge, wisdom, insight, and understanding.

He serves by seeking, and like my Heart Force Part, has Self-like energy.

He, like my Figure-Outer Part, can get activated and get in the way of the work I'm doing with other parts. They both mean well, but they want to analyze and find answers, which are important jobs but can stop or pull attention and energy from the other parts I'm working with.

My Seeker Part is in his twenties and is leaning forward to take information in, to learn, and he is holding a pad of paper with a pen poised over it ready to jot down what he learns.

Bob asks me to ask my Seeker Part to come sit beside me. He agrees.

With the Seeker less active I am able to spend time with the Heart Force Part, to be bask in the warm glow of its amber energy, to be loved and cared for, healed and renewed.

INSIGHTS

To be seen.

When someone recognizes something in us it's vital to remember that what they are recognizing is already in us. We have within us everything we need.

The experience of having another soul speak to our soul is truly profound, and the implications often go far beyond that single encounter. But as affirming and confirming as it is and can be, it's merely a recognition of something already inside us, and points to the truth that what most needs to happen is that we recognize and embrace it ourselves.

I've been guilty of thinking that I have enough love and strength to make any relationship work. I've been guilty of rushing into relationships with this sense of safety and security and then attempting to make them work by taking far too much responsibility for the other person and the relationship itself. But I've also seen that when I've stopped doing this, when I've let go, the great, gentle river of life carries me away or others away from me and restores peace and tranquility.

BOB'S NOTES

When I introduce IFS, I usually ask my client if they have seen the Pixar movie "Inside Out." Most of the movie takes place inside the mind of young girl. She is navigating leaving one world (the small Midwest town she grew up in) and moving to another world (the huge city of San Francisco). Inside her head you meet 5 characters (Parts); Joy, Sadness, Anger, Fear and Disgust. Each, in its own way, tries to protect the girl.

IFS introduces us to a new world and a new way of seeing the world.

We are all made up of stories. IFS tells us there can be many different perspectives of the same story...and that none of those perspectives is inherently "wrong" or "bad".

Just stay curious.

Invite.

Acknowledge.

Richard Schwartz wrote a book called "No Bad Parts." The belief that none of our Parts are bad is REVOLUTIONARY. This does not mean that there are no consequences to actions or that every behavior is acceptable. It means that the original INTENT of our Parts is good.

According to IFS, we have two types of Parts: Protectors and Exiles. We also have Self, but that is not a Part. It is our Essence.

The Exiles are the Parts of us (often young) who have experienced trauma. The Protectors try to keep the Exiles from hurting and being re-traumatized. Protectors are either Managers ("Never again will I let that happen") or Firefighters ("Make the hurting STOP").

Traumatized Parts deserve Protection. Protecting the vulnerable is honorable.

Good intentions. No Bad Parts.

Such a big, big heart.

Welcome Home.

SESSION FOUR

For the second week in a row the part that manifested, that was activated, was energy more than a being, presence more than persona.

In some ways this makes the part seem more nebulous, but also more spiritual, more entity than being, more like an Impressionist than Realist painting.

Bob and I usually spend the first part of the session talking and sharing, catching up. The parts work we do next often but not always flows from this discussion.

When nothing comes up during that preliminary chat, he'll ask something like, "Was there anything in particular you wanted to discuss today?"

I'll then share with him something I'm working on or some experience I had that activated parts that I'd like to explore.

It's at this point that we get curious.

Getting curious often begins with a body scan to see if the activated part(s) is residing in a particular place within in me.

Once the part or parts is identified we interact with it, engaging with curiosity and without judgment, exploring the parts age, job, beliefs, how it sees me, if it's burdened, and what it needs.

Today, while performing the body scan, I felt an energy in my chest strength.

When we got curiuos, I perceived the part as a force, an openness, a powerful part. There was also some tension present.

The part, which has a lot of self-like qualities, reveals that I have everything I need within me. The tension comes when I don't live that, when I look outside myself for what I need.

For far too long, I've been far too outward and others oriented. I'm an empath, sensitive to others, their moods and needs, and though I have spent my entire adult life going within and being inward focused, I've also spent far too much of it searching outside myself.

I'm a seeker and a thinker, a spiritual and creative introvert, so I've always had a rich interior life. I enjoy my own company and need daily doses of alone time. But I also crave connection, have wasted too much time caring what others think and trying to please and make them happy.

This season in my life is about a recalibration, a rebalancing, going within more, looking within more, and not just in my head but in my body and soul. This last, the balance between head and heart, mind and body, is another way I am out of balance and in need of a paradigm shift.

Bob and I talked about homecoming, about how I'm coming home to myself more than ever before.

My home is within me. That is where I must go. I am my home. That is what I must be.

Searching for a home outside of myself is foolish and futile. Asking another to be my home or attempting to be theirs. And I've done far too much of both—particularly the latter.

I care deeply for others, am often moved with compassion for those I encounter, and I never want that to change, but caring for others as opposed to caring about their approval and adulation is as different as lighting and a lighting bug.

I've been a pretty good home for myself over the years, but I have misguidedly tried to be a home for others, especially those close to me. I've felt and attempted to exert far too much responsibility for others, and in certain romantic, significant other relationships I've taken this to its most egregious extreme. I have attempted to save and rescue and be a home for and take responsibility for certain others and certain relationships, and this misguided and egotistical approach has made me feel something akin to heroic at times.

Love emanates from my Self, my soul, the divine spark of perfect love within me. And it's not just for me to give and share with others. It's for me. I can sit with it and fully experience it, and then maybe rather than taking actions that attempt to share it with others I can just be it and let that being, that presence emanate to others or not, spill out of me to others or not.

I also don't need a witness or someone to share an experience or thought or action with for it to be meaningful, profound or for it to ultimately matter.

Bob kept saying that I'm coming home, that I am home, and that the energy in my chest is what leads me to speak and write and create.

INSIGHTS

Home and homecoming are recurring themes during my first year of IFS.

As I was selling my home of 25 years and transitioning into a new one, I was also experiencing a spiritual and psychological homecoming of sorts.

In many ways, I was coming home to myself and realizing again that I was my home.

Outwardly, I was losing a longterm home and searching for another.

Inwardly, a similar process was happening. I was letting go (losing, if you will) any home that was outside of me, only coming home to Self (gaining, if you will) my true home.

Losing my outward orientation meant that I wasn't taking responsibility for others any longer—even my children and grandchildren, who I feel a tremendous responsibility for and always have. My children are grown and are responsible for themselves. They are their own homes. And my grandchildren have incredible loving and supportive parents. I am in their lives for love, for joy, for support, for care, and any assistance they may need, not to be responsible for them.

As long as I can remember, I have felt full of love and felt a responsibility to share it. I have been moved not only by compassion, but far too often by pity.

I have believed I was given so very much, and I was taught that "to whom much is given, much is required."

I have given out of my gratitude, which I feel good about, but I've also given out of guilt and responsibility.

I'm a firstborn, self-starter, from a family of hardworking responsible individuals, raised by micromanagers, and I've taken my sense of responsibility for others to extremes.

I'm a sensitive empath with a lot of love to give, and I have too often let caring turn to care-taking and responsibility turn to an over-responsibility for others.

Hi, my name is Michael, and I'm an over-responsible-holic with a bit of a savior complex, and a desire to be liked and respected, but I'm committed to recovery.

BOB'S NOTES

Between the ages of 18 and 22, I had the opportunity to be a camp counselor at a summer Methodist camp for high school students. It was called "Camp Colby." One summer, the man who started the camp back in the late 60s, came to do our campfire talks. He was Armenian and a wonderful story teller. He told the parables of Christ through the lens of the original culture. Sometimes they even had a rhythm.

At one of those campfires, mid-story, he had us repeat "It's what I hold that hold's me . . . It's what I hold that hold's me."

I got it in my bones.

He wasn't just talking about holding the people we love. He was talking about beliefs. The beliefs we hold also hold onto us.

We become attached to them.

Beliefs that we KNOW we have are powerful.

The ones we don't even know we carry are even MORE powerful.

In IFS, we recognize that Parts carry beliefs. Those beliefs direct how they function. Just like a relationship with a person, they more time we spend with Parts and the more we get to know them.

After this 4th session, Michael was reflecting on the belief of his Responsible part. He recognized how much that belief has held him. ("It's what I hold that holds me").

It went from being implicit, to being explicit.

Known.

Seen.

The beginning of a relationship.

SESSION FIVE

The night is dark and cool.

It had rained earlier and now the city lights refract off the damp and slick surfaces of asphalt, concrete, glass, and steel.

From an empty alleyway, a dark figure in a trench coat and fedora emerges carrying a small box.

He's a character straight out of film noir, a hardboiled detective, strong and tough, uncompromising and unrelenting, and he's on a case. The mysterious box he's carrying is small, white, and rectangular, and appears to be from a different era, perhaps even the future.

This is the first of many times that a Protector Part will appear as a detective or bodyguard or paramilitary operative.

Today I shared with Bob that I have been working on parts of me that hold pain—primarily the pain that comes from the words and actions of others, the slings and arrows, intended and not, of slights, cruelties, rejections, and betrayals.

In early life, like most sensitive empathic creatives, I took things far too personally and was prone to hurt feelings. Additionally, I had certain legacy parts that carried generational wounds and hurt feelings that had been handed down.

As I grew and matured, I learned that most if not all of what I had found hurtful had nothing to do with me, and my spiritual practices and self-development led me to healing and letting go. And though I was still sensitive, I was no longer part of the walking wounded, not easily hurt, not quickly offended.

But more recently I had opened my life to some truly toxic people and their dysfunctional dynamics, and though they were mostly out of my life and soon would be more or less completely, I was wanting to rid my system of the poison, heal from the wounds, and let go of any and all offense.

As Bob led me through getting curious, the detective/bodyguard protector part emerged holding a white rectangular box of grudges.

Activated by pain, his job was to protect a young, sensitive, innocent, and somewhat naive boy from pain, insult, and injury.

Bob had me ask him who he thought I was, he said he thought I was a small child with a big heart in need of protection.

Bob had me share with him who I really am—a grown man, a father and grandfather, who has no need of protection. I am calm and confident, strong and resilient.

He was surprised by who I am now and saw that I had no need of his protection.

I told him that holding onto pain and hurt and grudges, even locked in the white box, was actually hurting me.

I asked him if he would open the box and take them out.

He said he would.

When he opened the box, there were small scrolls inside, each rolled and tied with ribbon.

He was about to take out the scrolls, but before he could, each one transformed into a dove and flew up and away on their own.

Elegant, white doves flying up into a misty breaking dawn, soaring up above the cityscape.

I am filled with the such a sweet relief.

I am healed, pain free, and free free. I feel new and renewed, clean and original, open and unburdened, and now the—

An incessantly ringing phone.

Interruption.

Disruption.

As soon as I stop the ringing, it starts again.

This happens several times.

As this extraordinary experience was concluding, a family member called me repeatedly.

Each time I wouldn't accept the call, they called again. Over and over.

I believed I knew what it was about and it could wait, but I shared with Bob how distracted I felt.

Bob's brilliant response was for us to examine my distracted part.

The part of me who was most activated was the young, good boy part who attempts to please others and is deferential to authority figures. This part prefers not to upset or disappoint others, particularly those he perceives as important or in authority over him.

Another activated part, a teenage part in the role of older brother, speaks up and tells the younger, people pleaser part he's being annoying, that he needs to grow up and quit caring what anyone thinks.

Exposing both of these parts to Self, to love, safety, security, calmness, and compassion brings a serene acceptance and frees them from the burdens they carry.

I am reminded that there are no bad parts and every part has a job. But often the beliefs they carry about what that job is and how important it is often doesn't match current reality.

I do not need protection. I do not need to please or placate others. I do not need to say F you to everyone go at it alone. All three of the parts that were activated today just wanted to help, but they or at least their roles and their approach to them is no longer needed—if it ever was.

These parts, like all those I encounter on this journey are in need to let let Self care for them instead of the other way around.

INSIGHTS

I have lived a love-centered life.

My pursuit, my practice is love.

I was born in love, raised in love, and have spent a lifetime building on that firm foundation. All in love.

My sensitive, empathic nature means that I am able to experience compassionate love for others, to care for and be moved by them and their needs.

But this same nature means that I can be hurt, wounded by the unkindness and cruelty of others—especially since my practice is to live open-hearted, unencumbered by armor and shields.

And it's these very wounds and injuries that can block the flow of love.

As Rumi said, "Your task is not to seek for love, but merely to seek and find all the barriers within yourself that you have built against it."

The scrolls of hurt and pain and resentment in the white box were barriers to love. My task is to seek and find and remove them.

Opening the box, releasing the pain, brings serenity and restores the flow of love, like the elegant, upward flight of white doves.

BOB'S NOTES

A story about monkeys comes to mind.

In one of his trainings, Richard Schwartz tells a story about what happens when you go golfing in India (or maybe Malaysia, I don't remember). The courses are beautiful. Tropical. Lush.

But there's a catch. There are lots of monkeys on the golf courses.

You might hit a perfect drive, but when you come up to where you expected it to be, it is no longer there. A monkey grabbed it. So you have to go searching for your ball. Eventually you find it. The monkey dropped it somewhere.

So what do you do now? Do you try to get back to the spot where the ball first landed? Or do you just play where the monkey dropped the ball?

When we turn inward, we often carry memories or expectations of where we'd like to begin. Where the ball is "supposed to be." Usually, the harder we try to recapture it, the further it slips away.

In today's session, Michael was IN it. And then his phone kept interrupting. Another monkey. When he dropped back IN he was able to allow himself to begin with where that monkey dropped the ball.

We could have tried to go back. Reconnect with where he WAS. But in honoring his system's response to the monkey, we discovered something new. Another Part. And we began to get curious about it.

In IFS, we begin with whatever parts are present. Whatever and wherever the "monkey" happened to drop them. As we enter into the present, there may be other monkeys. Or even other balls.

It is helpful, or perhaps even necessary, to have someone with us who has a detached perspective of the golf course. To guide us. To help us choose what ball we might follow. To ask the monkeys to give us a little space. To remind us that we are playing on a course, but we are not the course itself.

SESSION SIX

Did my heart love till now? forswear it, sight! For I ne'er saw true beauty till this night.

O, she doth teach the torches to burn bright.

A young boy of eleven or twelve rushing home after school not wanting to miss the conclusion of Franco Zeffirelli's adaptation of *Romeo and Juliet* airing on TV.

It's all he's been able to think about since he had watched the first part the day before.

Innocent. Sensitive. Passionate. Romantic. On the cusp of adolescence, he can relate to the young lovers of Shakespeare's most famous and popular tragedy.

In all his short life he can't recall ever being moved as much, having his soul stirred as much as falling in love with Olivia Hussey's Juliet.

I have spent very little of my adult life not in a relationship.

In over 35 years of adulthood the time I've spent not in a relationship can probably be measured in months instead of years.

But for today's session, like every other one I've had with Bob so far, I'm single.

Happily, gratefully, single.

And it wasn't just that I was single and relieved and pleased to be so. I was comfortable and content.

For one of the few times in my life I'm not actively searching for a relationship.

My natural state, default setting, is to be in a relationship, sharing life with someone, caring for and being cared for by another.

Within the context of a good, healthy relationship I thrive. I have plenty of togetherness and separateness, continuing to pursue my spiritual growth and self-development and my vocations as a novelist, writer, teacher, counselor, speaker, and singer-songwriter.

I've also done these things in spite of the dynamics of unhealthy relationships with partners who weren't a good fit for me, but it requires so much more and places such an unnecessary strain on me—a burden I've always felt more than capable of bearing, but eventually, ultimately had to ask why I would. I was so busy seeing if I could clone a dinosaur I didn't stop to ask if I should.

I have been slow to end relationships I should've never started—or at least never let go as far or as long as they did. I've done this for a variety of reasons, but mostly because I wanted to be in a relationship and because I took on way too much responsibility for the other person and the relationship itself. And I did this so early in the process that by the time I saw more clearly the person's issues and realized they were ill-suited for me I already felt responsible for them. I've also always been a helper and a healer, a minister and a counselor, and did far too much of this, my vocation, in my relationships —far too often took my work home with me.

But no more.

Now, after attempting to make things work with ill-suited

and unhealthy partners, I am not only happily and contentedly single, but I won't repeat that pattern.

I share with Bob how something has shifted within me. Instead of wanting or needing or looking for a relationship, I am content and happy and embracing being single.

I told him it was hard to describe the depth of the change, but I felt it profoundly.

Unlike in previous periods of being single I didn't feel like anything was missing, didn't feel the need to be actively seeking someone. I'm in no way closed to a relationship, but I no longer feel the need to search for one, and I'm enjoying being single and absolutely loving the life I have.

My focus is within, not without. My primary and most important relationship is with my Self and not another. This process has been several years in the making and has led to a tectonic shift deep within me.

As we discus this, Bob asks if I have a lonely part.

And though it's not activated that I can tell we got curious.

The part I became aware of is a pre-teen little boy.

The young part recalls watching *Romeo and Juliet* as a kid and being so moved he got physically ill.

As far back as childhood he's wanted a relationship and spent much time back then daydreaming, imagining, longing. A seeker, he's always sought a soulmate in addition to everything else he was seeking. From a very young age he's wanted to experience an intense and intimate connection, to share life with and become one with another. And everything within his world—culture, romance, religion tells him that marriage is the ultimate end of this.

Interestingly, unsurprisingly, the most intense moments of loneliness he's experienced have been in relationships.

Always looking. Always seeking. Always searching.

His passionate romanticism causes him to idealize and

project onto others qualities and attributes that are simply not present.

His intuitive, often mystical journey through life has been one of valuing process above all else. As a creative and empath, he often feels his way through life. As a novelist, he's actively writing his own story. He's a discovery writer. He writes into the dark, trusting the process of creation. Part of this approach involves getting the plane in the air and then learning how to fly it, and he's far, far too often taken this same approach to relationships, believing he can figure it out and make it work once it's already in the air. This is coupled with other parts of his that are impatient and impulsive. Eventually, ultimately having to figure out how to land the plane and disembark because it was not the best flight for him.

Showing this part who I am now is transformational.

He is surprised and relieved and experiences a freedom and tranquility that only comes from letting a burden go.

The burden is the belief—in this case the belief that I needed someone else in order to experience complete fulfillment.

In the presence of Self, he is made whole, and sees not only am I complete and not in need of another, but he can let go of his heightened and extreme approach to his job of always looking, always seeking, always longing.

I let him know that I am so good and happy, so content and fulfilled, not missing anything, in need of nothing else, not a partner, not anything.

The experience of peace and contentment, of love and joy, is palpable.

INSIGHTS

I am so very grateful, feel so good about my life and growth.

It was interesting that Bob asked about my lonely part. I experienced some bouts of intense loneliness when I was a young man, the worst of them inside a relationship, but that has been a very long time ago.

I feel like I rarely experience loneliness these days, but that may be the difference in how I approach my aloneness, and my practice of looking within instead of without when anything, including loneliness, comes up.

I'm inspired by the words of Hafiz.

Don't surrender your loneliness so quickly. Let it cut you more deep. Let it ferment and season you as few humans and even divine ingredients can. Something missing in my heart tonight has made my eyes so soft, my voice so tender, my need for God absolutely clear.

When I do experience loneliness it's often momentary, and though it can be intense, I attempt to take Hafiz's advice to not surrender it too quickly.

I'm spending even more time alone these days, and I'm truly loving it. But I also feel somewhat displaced. I've just sold my home of 25 years. Most of what I own is in storage, and my living situation is temporary.

Recently, when I experienced some sadness and loneliness, I sat with it and embraced it. I let it bring me low—a beneficial experience because it's so different from my default settings.

I am in the process of letting go—of my previous life, my previous relationship that I rushed into while ignoring several red flags, my previous home, which was my home for longer than any other I've ever had, and certain friendships, which were more situational than I first thought.

Many, many things are up-in-the-air in my life right now. But I'm not. And I embrace the uncertainty and am reminded that it's always there, even when I don't perceive it as much as do in my current season of change and transition.

During this first year of IFS, I've read a number of helpful, instructive, and inspiring books, but none more so than "You Are the One You've Been Waiting For: Applying Internal Family Systems to Intimate Relationships" by the father of IFS, Richard Schwartz.

This profound work embodies all that I touched on in Session Six with Bob. It is bringing together of everything I have been seeing and learning and experiencing in regards to my relationships over the past decade or more.

Here is what the publisher says about this extraordinary book:

Do loving relationships end because couples lack communication skills, struggle to empathize, and fail to accommodate each other's needs? That's a common belief within and outside of the therapeutic world . . . but what if it's all wrong? In "You Are the One You've Been Waiting For," Dr. Richard Schwartz, the celebrated founder of Internal Family Systems (IFS) therapy, offers a new way—a path toward courageous love that replaces the striving, dependent, and disconnected approach to solving relationship challenges.

BOB'S NOTES

Another monkey story—this one about how you catch a monkey.

I don't remember where I heard this first.

To catch a monkey you need a gourd, strong twine, and a banana.

First you cut the gourd by the narrow end. Next you hollow it out. The opening in the gourd needs to be just wide enough for a monkey to slip in his hand. After you've done this, you tie the twine to the closed end of the gourd, ensuring that the twine holds fast. Finally you put the opened banana inside the gourd.

Once you have completed this you go into the jungle, find a spot where monkeys are known to reside, set the gourd out, and hide yourself behind a bush or a tree holding the other end of the twine firmly.

After some time, a monkey will eventually smell the banana. The monkey is hungry and curious. He finds the gourd, and after inspecting it puts his hand inside to pull out the banana.

But there's a problem.

When the monkey is holding the banana he is not able to slip his hand back out through the opening. Now you've got him.

You can begin pulling him in. Try as he might he can't escape.

Unless...

He lets go of the banana.

But he's hungry. And it's really, really hard to decide to let go.

Choices.

What are we holding?

How is it holding us?

As Michael shared, for many of us the hardest thing to let go of is another person. Or more accurately, what that person represents to some of our Parts. What Parts are drawn out. What Parts NEED something. Are SEEKING for something.

In IFS, we find the Part/s that want to hold. They are not bad. They are not wrong. They are just trying to protect another Part of us.

How old are they? Who do they think we are? Can we introduce them to ourSelves as we are today? How do they respond to that? How do we feel towards these Parts that are working hard to protect who they think we are?

We often find compassion, connection, calm. This is Self Energy.

We are softly lead back to the truth. We are the one's we're looking for.

SESSION SEVEN

A bright, mid-morning in New York, the sun glinting off the glass of tall buildings and the yellow taxis on the busy streets below.

An enormous and storied 5th Avenue department store straight out of a movie, the surfaces of its counters and displays polished to perfection.

A few minutes before opening, and each department immaculate. Everything sparkles and shines. Everything smells as new as unworn leather and unwashed dye.

The perfume counter smells like a fragrant flower garden in full bloom.

The mirrors atop the makeup counters gleam and reflect the bright, but flattering lights surrounding them.

Behind the scenes, in a part of the store no customer ever sees—a storage, warehouse, workroom—a morning meeting is taking place.

In my session with Bob today I share with him how I'm working on those parts of me that stay too busy, that work too much, that are impatient and are almost always in a hurry.

I'm a novelist and writer, who during a 25-year career has produced over 50 books. People often comment on how consistent and prolific I am, and wonder how I can have such a rich full life and enjoy so many other activities—time with family, playing with grandchildren, making music, giving inspirational talks, hanging with friends, and so much more—and still produce so much.

In many ways, my outward life is slow and quiet and simple —by design, so my inner life can be fast-paced, creative, and complex.

And though I have no desire to decrease the rich, creative life of my mind, I do want to unburden the parts of me who rush around and rarely rest.

When we get curious, my productive parts present as the department heads of a large New York City department store.

The store seems like it has been part of the fabric of the city almost as long as there has been a city. It's the beating heart of the pounding pulse of the city, the streets leading to it the arteries and veins carrying the oxygenated blood of customers with money to and from its doors.

The grand, opulent store is a showpiece of the city, and is obviously well-run, expertly managed, and operated with precision.

This morning the departments heads are meeting with a manager of sorts in rustic warehouse storage space.

Of the ten or so heads of departments, none stand out more than the managers of the mens and women's clothing.

Their stylish yet classic clothes, crisply pressed and pristine, fit their tall, lean, muscular bodies as if they were tailored for them instead of off the racks of their departments.

They, like the other parts, are very good at what they do. The are smart, competent, driven, organized, serious, and often come across as aloof or distracted.

They stand with the other department head parts in front

of the manager, who is an older man and a tailor. His suit coat is off and his measuring tape is draped around his neck. He stands behind a large wooden work station, the tools of his trade—fabric, needles, threads, scissors, chalk—strewn about it.

The department head parts are standing though there are chairs. They are impatient, anxious to return to the work they were pulled away from for the meeting, and the tailor/manager part isn't any more enthused about the setting than they are.

However, since they are here, they share with him their gripes and grievances, wanting him to take care of and fix them.

Bob asks if I can go meet with them.

When Self enters the room, everyone immediately recognizes him as the owner and boss and react accordingly with respect and deference. And though they still want to get back on the floor and do a good job for him, they are not as impatient as they were—and certainly don't show it.

I let everyone know how much I appreciate the job they are doing, but also let them know I'd like to change the work environment, making it more relaxed, less rushed, less stressed.

I ask them to take a seat and let them know that it's okay if they don't make it back to their department before the store opens.

They sit and a relaxed calm comes over everyone.

The Tailor Part says he would prefer not to be a manager, that he really just wants to work as a tailor, creating clothes instead of managing others.

I let him know that is absolutely fine.

I then tell the Department Head Parts to bring any issues they have directly to me.

This gives them an even greater sense of calm and confidence and peace.

As they sit there I ask them to be even more still, more

relaxed, and receive the calm, compassionate energy from my Self.

They do.

Stillness. Serenity. Tranquility.

Now no one is in a hurry to leave.

INSIGHTS

Rumi's Guest House in this instance was a New York Department Store.

My manager parts have manager parts.

There was a heightened sense of mortality, a ticking clock counting down, causing my parts to believe time is running out and that they better get as much done as soon and as quickly as possible.

Every part has a job. And all but the Tailor Part wanted and needed to keep theirs—just with a different, more calm and peaceful approach. And, in fact, the Tailor kept his, just let go of the added responsibility that wasn't his to begin with.

The beliefs my parts held—that time was running out, that they had to rush and work around the clock—was what burdened them. Now they work in a more clam and serene way, still doing their important and vital jobs, but without the toxic beliefs that robbed them of peace and joy.

BOB'S NOTES

The Heart, the Hope, the Foundation of IFS is SELF. It allows everything else space to BE as it is. It is unconditional and transcendent.

I attended the Taoist Sanctuary in San Diego and practiced Tai Chi throughout my 20s. Both the Sanctuary and the practice were a safe place. Containers when so much felt uncontainable.

The practice of Tai Chi is a process of continually coming up against where you are holding. It begins with the challenges within our physical form and moves to connecting with other aspects (Parts) of us.

Taoism became a grounding model for me. I sought balance and harmony, and it helped me make sense of the energy of some of my extremes. My Yin and my Yang. And the awareness that within each is the other.

The *Tao Te Ching* is a guidebook. A pointer.

Verse 1 (translation by Stephen Mitchell's-1995):

The tao that can be told if not the eternal Tao.
The name that can be named is not the eternal Name.

The unnamable is the eternally real.
Naming is the origin of all particular things.
Free from desire, you realize the mystery.
Caught in desire, you only see the manifestations.
Yet mystery and manifestations arise from the same source.
This source is darkness.
Darkness within darkness.
The gateway to all understanding.

In IFS, they say is you can SEE a part, then it is not Self. Self is not experiencED, it is the ExperienCOR. What Michael described is probably what we call a Self-like Part.

I imagine Self-like Parts being an idealized image. Nameable. Pointing the way, but not the Way.

As much as I want to describe/name/identify SELF, I can't.

Richard Schwartz has 8 "Cs" to describe the energy of SELF. They are Curiosity, Calm, Compassion, Courage, Clarity, Creativity, Confidence, and Connected. I have felt/been in/experienced these. Could this be what Michael was experiencing?

SESSION EIGHT

Through tear-smeared vision, everything is soft and shimmery, radiantly refracting light.

Eyes red and stinging.

Heart hurting and sad.

My liquid-tinted vision gives everything an otherworldly and ghostly appearance, and causes apparitions to float across the foreground.

At first I see an evidence locker, everything organized and neat, held in paper and plastic bags and cardboard boxes—all with labels bearing bright red block letters adhering to them.

The smallish evidence room transforms into a larger historical room inside a library where a place's and a people's past is remembered and recalled, stored and preserved.

Today, as I get curious and scan my body, I discover pain and sadness.

I'm haunted by past insults and injuries, mistakes and failures, those times I hurt and was hurt by others.

I begin to see how these painful memories are stored, locked in my mind and body, held in evidence for my accusatory Prosector Part to use against me.

As I continue to scan and explore with calm curiosity, I enter a historical room inside a library.

The librarian emerges and becomes visible, and I can see that he appears flowy and ghostly.

This apparition librarian part is known as The Keeper and is the manager of my emotional memory archives.

Are these are exiles? They probably are, but for now they don't present as parts. Perhaps because the focus is on The Keeper.

I show him who I am now and let him know I don't need protection from any memories or feelings, painful or otherwise. I let him know I see each one as valuable, a treasured experience, a teacher, a guide.

Bob asks why they have to be locked in a room, and I ask The Keeper if he'll agree to keep the door unlocked and open.

Bob then asks why they have to be in a room at all, and I ask The Keeper to set them free.

Their release is a release of pain and shame, belief and burden, guilt and grievance.

As they become free, I see that the library is actually underwater, and the Keeper is floating in the water, less of a ghost and more of a swimmer.

The new freedom—for both the emotional memories and The Keeper—floods the watery library with a warm, golden glow that has incredible properties including a calm but powerful beauty.

I then realize that they are all in a womb, floating in embryonic fluid, and that this is my Heart Library.

BOB'S NOTES

Many folks come to therapy because they are experiencing some form of internal chaos. "Blending" is the term IFS uses to describe many Parts being activated at the same time. Chaos.

With IFS we begin with Curiosity. As we become curious, Parts often soften the force of their protective edge. They begin to "unblend." They experience Calm and begin feeling Connected to us. As they unblend, we are able to get to see them with more Clarity. They become known and often feel our Compassion. This is a Creative process that takes Courage. As we engage in over and over again. We gain Confidence.

The eight C's of Self energy.

In this session, Michael spoke about "freedom." So, what is the difference between freedom and chaos?

By his accounts, Michael's Parts were unblending (no longer chaotic) and experiencing his Self energy. In the process they began to unburden themselves.

In IFS, beliefs are the burdens. "Unburdening" is a final step in freeing Parts (often Exiles) from the beliefs that have been holding them.

Some of these beliefs might include:

I'm defective.
I'm out of control.
I'm forever bad.
I'll never be enough.
I'm in darkness.
I am darkness.

What might it be like to be freed from such burdens? To no longer carry such beliefs. To be in amazing grace.

"I once was lost, but now am found.
Was blind but now I see."

SESSION NINE

Evening. In the gloaming.
    Two lovers sitting in a swing by a secluded lake.
    The last of the setting sun burnishing the rust-colored tips of the pines on the western rim of the lake.
    The woman places her head on the man's shoulder and her hand over his heart.
    "You're the most gentle man I've ever known. Thank you for ... being so patient with me. I'm sorry again for my ... episode. I'm gonna get better. I'm gonna make it up to you. I ... promise. Even when I'm having my meltdowns ... you make me feel ... so safe, so ... Well, actually, I don't feel safe during them. But afterwards when I'm able to ... when I can think clearly again ... I realize how hateful I was and ... Thank you for not ... acting like I do during those times. I'm so grateful ... So in love with you. You know you're my dream come true ... the great love of my life."
    Rumi comes to mind.

Lovers find secret places
inside this violent world
where they make transactions

with beauty.

But what happens when that violence is not in the world but in the wounded, traumatized, unhealed and un-liberated parts and unattached burdens, of one or both of the lovers?

On the drive home from the lake. The woman in the passenger seat, scrolling on her phone.

"Why would you post that picture of us?" she asks.

He can hear the raw, ragged rage in her voice. She's entering one of her episodes and he knows there's nothing he can do about it.

"Which—"

"You did that on purpose to make me look fat?"

"*What*?"

"You did. You made me look ever fatter than I am."

"You're not fat and I didn't—"

He knows there's nothing he can say to reason with her, but there's a part of him that always tries, that believes he can reach her, can find inside her the Self or at least the kinder, more loving parts.

"How'd you do it? With the fat girlfriend app?"

Part of him, a part that said it would never again be surprised by anything she says, no matter how outrageous, is shocked.

"*The what?*"

It's so absurd, so outlandish, yet so real to her.

It'd be comical if it weren't so tragic. She's dead serious, delirious with irrational rage.

Part of him is so weary of this cycle, so ready for it to end like she's promised over and over that it would. Part of him takes it personally and believes it's so unfair, that he doesn't deserve this. Another part of him is frustrated, irritated, and angry.

"Listen to yourself," he says. "There's no such thing as the fat girlfriend app. You're being . . . This is crazy."

He realizes that not only should he not be trying to reason with her, but he certainly shouldn't be using words like *crazy*.

"I'm not crazy."

"I didn't say *you* were. I said this is crazy. But it was a poor choice of words. I should've said irrational or unreal or—"

Of course, he shouldn't have said anything along those lines.

"You always try to make me feel crazy, try to put me down and—"

"That's not true. Please. Listen to what you're saying."

If this continues to escalate and turns into one of her major meltdowns, it will only get worse, it will go on for days, and she will say the most cruel and hateful things she can think of. And it will be the eighth time in as many months.

"This is so . . . surreal," he says. "Remember when this happened the last time? You said it would never happen again. You said if it did to remind you that—"

"Stop the car. I want to get out."

"*What? No.*"

"Stop the fuckin' car right now or I'll jump out."

"Are you serious?"

She grabs the door handle and he knows in the state she's in she might just do it.

He slows the car down and pulls the car onto the shoulder of the road.

"Please don't get out. I won' talk anymore. I'll just sit here with you. At least let me drive you home."

"I don't have a home. It's your home. It's your life. It's your family. It's your friends. I'm . . . I'm not living like this anymore. I'm not going to be the Robin to your Batman, the Judas to your Jesus. I'm done."

These episodes, outbursts, meltdowns are getting worse

and more frequent. He's tried to help her, to save her, to forgive and forget and restore some sort of equilibrium after the storm passes, but he knows any break in the storm is temporary. He's tried everything he knows to do, and is beginning to realize there's nothing he can do. He can't save her. He can't love her enough to fill the blackhole inside her. Only she can do for herself what needs to be done. He feels responsible for her and for the relationship. But he's realizing he can't be. He should've never tried to be. As difficult as it is, he has to tell his overly-responsible part to stand aside, to let go, to only take responsibility for himself and no one else.

Other parts get activated and feel shame and failure and anger.

Today in my session with Bob, I share with him how I'm dealing with my angry and judgmental parts—especially those angry and upset at a previous partner.

I want to deal with their hostility toward her and be free from it.

Bob says he senses that the angry part is still attached to the previous partner who I'm angry with.

I get curious about that.

I have been going through the process of letting go—of attachment and responsibility and resentment and expectation and a million other things—and see that my anger is a conduit that continues to connect the angry part to her.

When the relationship ended, I immediately felt a sense of relief. I had suffered through a level of verbal cruelty toward me and those I love that I never could've imagined. I had believed that with enough love and understanding, kindness and compassion, healing would take place and her episodes would end. But they never did. They only got worse. I felt I had done all I could do to love and care for my partner, but knew only she could do the work of healing that she needed. When we decided to end the relationship, I was so grateful to never again have to undergo her outlandish and vicious attacks. I felt many things, of course, including shame and embarrassment, but also gratitude and release. All of this was nearly instant. However, the process of healing and processing and letting go of attachment and responsibility and expectations is still ongoing, and I see how the hurt and angry and caring and judgmental and resentful parts are still tethered to the partner by those very feelings.

Bob asks if part of me thinks I shouldn't be angry at my previous partner.

And I definitely do have a part that believes that.

Part of me believes that I should never be anything but loving, that I should see everyone's behavior, no matter how extreme or hateful, as unhealed and unburdened parts, and only respond with kindness and compassion.

Another part of me responds by attempting to take responsibility for others and help them heal.

Bob then asks if I have a part that thinks I should never get angry—at anyone for anything.

And I do have such a part—or at least one who feels something similar to that, who expects and demands a certain kind of moral perfectionism and idealism that doesn't involve anger.

When I was younger, and to a lesser extent as I got older, this part, when activated, has prevented me from creating and maintaining certain boundaries that are absolutely necessary for an empath to have peaceful and serene relationships. Having such boundaries is part of what led to the necessary and inevitable end of this particular relationship.

I tell Bob I don't want any part of me attached to the previous partner, and I don't want any part of me angry or resentful or upset with her or anyone else.

I then recall a certain compulsive behavior of hers that part of me still thinks about with criticism and judgement—and anger.

This leads to recalling more of the outlandish accusations against me, my family, and friends. Each and everyone absurd and preposterous and objectively not true, but nonetheless toxic and hurtful.

Bob asks me to invite the angry parts to join Self in a safe place.

I sit in circle with them on the beach next to the Gulf in the evening as the sun is setting and a calm descends with the softening of the light.

My Self energy comforts and calms and heals the parts. They let go of their anger and attachment and through this process of release are restored to wholeness and freedom.

And this, like all my IFS parts work, is a far more profound and deeper experience than I can explain or describe.

INSIGHTS

I don't often get angry, but I get angry more often than I express it.

On those rare occasions when I feel and express anger, I'm not comfortable with how I feel and act, nor how others respond to it, especially those close to me.

Much of what is expressed as anger, especially in men, is pain, but they are more comfortable expressing anger than emotional pain or hurt feelings.

I felt judgement and anger at my previous partner when we were together and she was saying and doing the hurtful and harmful thing she was. And each time I went through a process of letting it go, of processing and forgiving, but when the relationship was over I found I had more processing to do—something IFS helped me do at deeper level.

During and after the relationship, my Seeker/Figure-Outer Part searched for the causes for her toxic behaviors, but all answers—trauma, mental illness, addiction, legacy and unattached burdens—no matter how applicable, are ultimately unsatisfactory, only marginally helpful, and sort of beside the point.

I have used them in the past to gain insight, understanding, and compassion, and as helpful and beneficial in some ways as that was, it never got me to the ultimate place of surrender, release, and unburdening that IFS has.

BOB'S NOTES

I remember one of my early sessions with my therapist, Marshall. I was 21 years old. He asked me, "What is the opposite of love?" Like most, I responded with "hate," but I was wrong.

The opposite of love is indifference. It's the opposite of holding on, because you don't even notice.

As I began my vocation as a social worker, Marshall gave me a book titled, "Relationship, The Heart of Helping People" by Helen Harris Perlman. It has reminded me that, when it comes down to it, the most valuable tool I have is how I honor the relationship I have with each other my clients.

Of course boundaries are necessary, but too often therapists allow boundary to keep them (or protect them) from having a human to human relationship with their clients.

My dad is still my hero. Always has been. I'm lucky.

Dad worked as an insurance agent for close to 40 years. But that's not who he was. My dad was someone that people liked to sit down with and just "bullshit" (as he might say). It might be about insurance, or family, or issues of the day. It didn't matter. People knew my dad cared. He listened. He was present.

And that's who I've always wanted to be. I'm grateful I have the privilege to hear people's story and be given their trust.

In IFS, relationship is also at the heart. The difference (or similarity) is that it's about the relationships inside of us.

Nothing draws out Parts out like the dynamics within our most intimate relationships. This fertile ground is what lead Michael to reach out to me.

In this session he allowed himself to revisit this recent relationship and many of the Parts that had been stirred—blended. Something in him knew they wouldn't truly go away, but would only manifest again in new relationships. He needed to spend some time with them. Sit down with them and listen.

Eventually find that space where they could just "bullshit" with each other.

SESSION TEN

I have a confession to make.
   A dirty little secret to share.
   We'll get to that, but first...
   Before I encountered IFS, I conceived of myself more or less as a monolithic being. Sure, I'd refer to different aspects of my being by different names—mind, brain, body, heart, soul—but I essentially saw myself as a single self.
   And the way I saw that self was as a very good human being. Sure, I had shit I was working on—always had been, always would be—but I was gentle and kind and compassionate and creative and loving. I would've said I was a great dad and grandude and a good friend, son, partner. And though I saw myself as good, I was also always trying to be better—to grow and evolve and become an ongoing a better iteration of my self.
   IFS changed all that.
   I still see my self as a good person, and in some ways I see myself as far better than I did before. I see my Self as complete and and compassionate and kind and loving and calm—and that's the way I see yours.

But unlike before I see my being as multi instead of mono, a rich mosaic instead of a single stone, a family instead of an individual, a universe or even multiverse instead of a single organism.

I have parts. Many of them.

And seeing my being this way is not all that different than other formulations such as id, ego, superego, or unconscious, subconscious, conscious, collective unconscious, or body, soul, spirit, or inner child. I just happen to believe the IFS model is more accurate, more in line with my lived experience.

Parts of me want to be perfect. Not just good, but great. Heroic. Fully and completely kind and loving and wise. For them good is not good enough. They want to be the best—the best dad, the best son, the best partner, the best friend, the best novelist, the best speaker, the best songwriter.

And here's my confession, my dirty little secret.

Parts of me absolutely, positively do not want to acknowledge or admit that other parts of me can be unkind, unloving, petty, selfish, self-centered, and any number of other attributes they find not just distasteful but downright deplorable.

That's why I mentioned seeing myself as a good human being. It has always been a part of my identity, so of course parts of me don't want to view me as anything but that.

I share with Bob how I want to do parts work on these parts —the ones don't want to acknowledge the darker parts of me, the parts that can't bring themselves to cop to imperfection, to being critical or judgmental or selfish.

When I get curious I encounter a sweet, sensitive Little Boy Part who is shamed by an authority figure for doing something other than what is seen by family, culture, and religion as acceptable.

Though the inflation was tiny and ultimately insignificant, and the correction was relatively gentle and mild, the little boy took the correction to heart and felt more shame than the authority figure could've never imagined.

When someone in authority—parents, teachers, coaches, ministers—tells the little boy what is and is not acceptable, he embraces it like only a sensitive true believer and people-pleaser can.

A Teenager Part comes forward and tells the Little Boy Part not to sweat it. It's no big deal. Who cares what the old people think? Who cares what anyone else thinks? Don't live by society and family and religion's conventions and warped sense of right and wrong.

Rumi springs to mind.

Out beyond ideas of wrongdoing and rightdoing there is a field. I'll meet you there. When the soul lies down in that grass the world is too full to talk about.

Another part, a Self-like Peacemaker Part begins to comfort both parts, reassuring and validating them both, attempting to bring harmony.

Bob asks me if I'd like to take these parts somewhere to sit with me.

I choose a place in the woods that was sacred to me, a place that development put on the ropes, then Hurricane Michael finished off.

This spot, inside the old State Park, was where I went to meditate, contemplate, be still and quiet, when I was teenager and young man.

I sat with my parts on a pine tree-covered hill at the upper end of a slight ridge, sloping down to a pond.

The Little Boy Part begins to release the tension of perfectionism and people-pleasing and the need to comply and obey, while the Teenager Part releases his rejection of and disdain for what he sees as weak sheeple. Both parts relax, and are permeated by an empowering, freeing, healing, energy flowing from me to them.

The Self-like Part tells them that the parts that are judging them are just other parts in need of releasing burdens, in need of unblending, which they will do as we continue this work. And these part aren't a reflection on them or Self, and they don't need to try to please them or react to them in any way.

INSIGHTS

Though this parts work session didn't get directly to the parts of me that don't want to admit other parts of me can be undesirable shits, I think it began the process and paved the way to get there, and, of course, just acknowledging them did a lot toward the work that needs to be done.

Following the session, Bob texted me something that came out of a similar session he had this week. *In its efforts to keep my vulnerable parts safe, my self-like part blocks them from truly experiencing/trusting me.*

I feel like my primary job right now is working on myself, developing myself, addressing, healing, growing—and the novel writing and songwriting and other work activities are secondary. I've always done both in differing percentages, but for now this is my most important job.

I feel so fortunate to be able to do the work. I'm very grateful for where I am in life and in this current transition. So many opportunities. So very grateful. Thanks you! Teach me. Direct me. Help me.

I am home. I am the center that holds. I am calm and

creative and curious and compassionate and caring and generous and wise and insightful and kind.

My Self is the calm center in any storm, my home. From it flows everything, whether to me or others, and what flows from it is beyond words.

To this Bob responded "The Tao that can be named is not the Tao."

It is one of my favorite sayings from the *Tao Te Ching*, and serves as yet another confirmation that Bob is the perfect counselor for me.

I agreed with his quoting about the Tao and added what Rumi said, "The language of God is silence. All else is poor transition."

BOB'S NOTES

In this session Michael gives attention and space to some of his paradoxes.

When I can embrace paradox, I am most at peace. IFS gives permission for paradox. It even encourages and nurtures it.

Michael loves Rumi. I find Truth in Walt Whitman. During a creative and vibrant time in my early 20s, Whitman was like a brother. Verses from "Leaves of Grass" spoke to my soul. They gave me permission to be a paradox.

"Do I contradict myself? Very well then I contradict myself. I am large. I contain multitudes."

I can be perfect and imperfect at the same time. I can be brave and scared, angry and peaceful, young and old, serious and silly, and on and on and on.

Alanis Morissette wrote the Introduction to Richard Schwartz's book "No Bad Parts: Healing Trauma and Restoring Wholeness with the Internal Family Systems Model."

She also sang and wrote the lyrics to "Hand in My Pocket." Its lyrics are a love song of paradox.

Have a listen.

SESSION ELEVEN

Sunday morning in the South.
Circa 1976.
Small town. Empty streets. Everything closed save the one convenient store in town where your mom can send you to buy her a new pair of pantyhose in a plastic egg before church—and you an Icee and Butterfinger for your trouble—but where the worse wino in town can't get anything to help him because it's illegal to sell liquor on Sundays.
Like most small Southern towns, there are more churches than anything else, and this morning, each one—those white Protestant Mainline ones on Main Street, those backwoods tongue-talking ones, and those black ones confined by an unspoken and unofficial segregation—hold most of the town's people inside, their large, gas-guzzling behemoth vehicles waiting outside on dirt and grass parking lots.
In a small Sunday school room cooled by a noisy window unit and smelling faintly of mildew in a redbrick Methodist Church building a little boy sits in a hard metal folding chair in a circle with other kids and a middle-aged teacher. He's holding

his small Children's Living Bible, the one with his name engraved in gold on the hardcover, on his lap, and he has a crinkled dollar in his pocket for when the offering plate is passed.

He looks lovingly of the picture of white Jesus with a lamb draped over his shoulders hanging crookedly on the wall and answers the questions the teacher asks with earnest piety.

Today Bob and I talk about and do work with my Inner Critic Parts.

I share with him how I don't often hear from them and how, in spite of them, I've for the most part lived according to my own convictions, traveled my own path to the rhythm of my own percussionist, not allowing them influence or control. But I'd like to understand them better, explore their motivation, and, if not, silence at least soothe and de-activate them.

When I get curious, I encounter some Parental and Teacher and Parishioner Parts.

Interestingly, these parts have been some of the most loving and supportive parts in my life. They genuinely love and adore me. They are all older females from my childhood—a Mother Part, a Sunday School Teacher Part, and the parishioner who was my number one fan and supporter from my first parish when I was a young minister.

I share with Bob how truly loved and supported I feel by these parts, and how much I love and care for them.

He asks how they see me.

They each saw me as young and innocent and in need of protection. The Sunday School Teacher Part saw me as around ten and the Parishioner Part saw me as 22.

Each of the parts are motivated by care and concern and genuine affection and don't believe that anything they say is in any way critical. To them it's just expressions of experience and wisdom and their way of looking out for me. It's their way of protecting a young, vulnerable me, especially in regards to how

I'm perceived by others. They are outwardly oriented and care what others think and want me to be perceived in the best possible way.

They are deeply entrenched in a community and culture and know and care what is expected. They can see that I am not a part of their group in the same way and they want to help me be. They are well-meaning and are holding up a certain standard they have for me, an expectation, a certain perfectionism they believe I am capable of.

When Bob asks me how I feel toward them, I let him know how much I love and appreciate them, which is part of the issue—because the Little Boy Part of me in some ways wants to please them and not let them down.

There's a Teenager Part who doesn't listen to them, who rejects the culture and religion they represent. And he tells the Little Boy Part he should do the same—not care at all what they think, what anybody thinks.

Bob asks me if I'd like to take the Critic/Protector Parts somewhere and sit with them.

I take them to a small secluded lake our family owns and sit with them in a circle around a fire.

I speak with them and show them who I am now.

They see that I am their age and even older.

They can see I need less of their protection and criticisms, but they are not yet willing to stop completely.

I let them know that I have no need of their protection and criticism, and that I can do that for myself, that my Self has everything I need.

Another Part of me tells them that whatever external standards they have for me, my internal ones, the ones that emanate from my true, authentic Self, are more in every way—more loving, more moral, more kind and compassionate, more honest, more creative and productive.

Bob asks if these parts can do a different job.

Each part in its turn, transitions from critic to assistant.

All the parts get so excited about the possibilities of their new tasks. They feel free and creative and begin to see how they can work with and help other parts to accomplish so much.

INSIGHTS

I found it fascinating that my critics were parts who loved and cared for me and that their criticism was motivated by a genuine care for me.

This dynamic lent their voices credibility and gave them power they wouldn't have had if they had been more uncaring critics.

Because of their love and care, because of the place they held for me in younger life, my Little Boy Part wanted to please them, even as other parts of me were rejecting their standards and criticisms.

When we are young and vulnerable and parents and other authorities seem godlike in their all-knowing, we lack the experience, knowledge, wisdom, and defenses to properly question the indoctrination that is taking place. And it doesn't just come from them—but from every quarter of culture.

BOB'S NOTES

Today one of my clients was telling me about her experience of shame. How she heard it and FELT it when she was young, and how she carries it today. We proceeded to talk about the difference between shame and guilt.

Guilt is focused on a behavior. You DID something you should not have done.

Shame is focused on BEING. You ARE something wrong.

It's difficult for many of us to discern between shame and guilt.

We have some experience of what Michael calls an Inner Critic, but all we know is IT's voice. Or perhaps we have difference types of Parts that carry the energy of a Critic and we're confused.

A common theory is that we carry the voices of our parents or caregivers inside of us. We may also carry the voices of influential people in our lives (for better or worse) along the way: a coach, teacher, minister, friend, or relative. These voices may even be larger than individuals and carry the beliefs of a family, religion, community, culture, etc.

These voices and beliefs get attached to Parts. And this is where we come to shame and guilt.

For Michael, his "Inner Critic" seems to primarily use guilt and focus on his actions. For some of us, the "Inner Critic" is a voice of shame telling us we ARE flawed, less than, or just plain bad. And if that is who we ARE, how do we get away from ourselves?

This double bind is the trapped and stuck feeling many bring with them into therapy.

In IFS, a "Legacy" is a belief that is passed down from the past. It is ours now, but we didn't cause or create it.

I have found freedom in this understanding that I am not the cause of some of the beliefs of my Parts. It's even allowed me to extend forgiveness to those who passed it along to me....because it was also passed along to them. And this awareness has allowed me to have more compassion for my Firefighter parts, because they are just trying to make IT stop, and take me away....from ME.

The illusion is that I AM this Legacy. But I am NOT. And once I have some space (unblending) from it, I can see that I am not longer IT. IT is just a Part of me. I am a SELF that is expansive and infinite and so much larger than any Part.

SESSION TWELVE

I'm experiencing more freedom and serenity than I have in a long time.

Adding IFS work with Bob to my other spiritual, intellectual and psychological practices and pursuits has not only brought about release and healing and insight, but has also amplified and magnified the efficacy of my other practices.

I've believed in and practiced the talking cure of talk therapy for many, many years, and though I still value it, I'm finding IFS parts work far and away more beneficial. It's not only a great fit for me, but the practice of it reaches depths and accesses aspects of me like nothing else ever has.

I encountered a former student at one of my recent book signings, and she commented that there was something different about me and that I looked happier than the last time she saw me, which had been a few years.

I found this very interesting because I don't feel happier. However, I do feel more far more free than the last time she saw me. And I believe it to be in two primary ways.

The last time she saw me I was in a relationship with someone where I was working very hard to make it work instead of doing what I need to do, which was let it go. She wasn't the first or last person that said I looked happier and freer after I finally ended that relationship.

I believe the other reason for the difference perceived and the happiness she observed is a result of the IFS work I'm doing with Bob.

When I share this with Bob he says she's probably seeing the unblending of my parts and the freedom and serenity that results from it.

Being Self-led and inward-oriented means I neither look for nor need recognition or validation from others, from outside of myself. And yet, having others notice and comment serves as confirmation for what I already know, which is nice.

I knew I was a novelist long before anyone else did.

I had to know before anyone else could.

I practiced my craft and wrote every day for three years before my first book was published. The book being published didn't make me a novelist, writing a novel did. The published novel let everyone see (and hold and read) what was already true.

The work is the reward, the cake. Everything else is icing.

I love the process of writing a novel or a book or a song, not just the finished product.

I love doing parts work and I know the profound impact it's having on me. Others noticing is nice but not necessary.

BOB'S NOTES

In a session when I'm describing blending and unblending I do the following:

I place my hands in front of me, palms towards my chest like I'm holding something.

I first move my hands towards each other, gradually linking my fingers together until my hands are clasped.

Next I gradually pull them apart.

At first I go slowly and then do it more quickly and with force.

Try this. Allow yourself to FEEL it. Imagine your Protectors doing this....all in effort to keep other Parts of you safe. Notice their good intent. Perhaps even extend appreciation to them for their efforts.

Blending is not bad. It is protective.

Allow yourself to be curious.

SESSION THIRTEEN

She's a two-year-old blue-eyed beauty, brilliant and imaginative and creative.

She's the daughter of his daughter, and he loves and cares for her the way he did his daughter, only with the added patience and presence of and older man.

He looks forward to the days when he gets to keep her, visits her on the days other family members keep her.

She calls him Grandu, which is short for Grandude, and the way she says it with her sweet, little voice, absolutely melts him.

This morning, like every morning they're together, they have played and pretended and had the best time.

They've played laundry basket spaceship, zoo, hide-n-seek, toilet paper Olympics, stuffed animal search and rescue, ice cream shop, and had several Disney Princess tea party.

He's made her favorite food for lunch—Mac & Cheese—he's held her, read to her, told her he loves her about a billion times, he's changed her, and now it's . . .

Nap time.

Dreaded nap time.

The moment he begins to turn off and dim the lights, she asks what he's doing—asks knowingly, asks accusingly.

"We're gonna take just a little rest, so we feel like playing the rest of the afternoon," he says. "Jus a short one. And then we'll play, play, play until your mommy picks you up."

He turns on the fan as she begins to whimper.

When he lifts her and moves toward the hallway, she begins to cry.

Holding her close, he asks her to lay her little head on his shoulder and close her eyes, as he moved up and down the dim hallway, singing to her.

"Hush little baby, don't say a word, Grandu's gonna buy you a mocking bird."

She squirms and wiggles and cries and talks, anything to stay awake.

She pleads and bargains.

She resists.

She resists and resists and resists.

Until . . .

She's fast asleep on her Grandu's shoulder.

He then eases into the recliner with her, and for the next hour-and-a-half she sleeps on his chest, her head on his shoulder, their hearts beating next to each other's.

Today in my session with Bob I get curious about some parts of me feeling some dread, anxiety, and overwhelm about the number of events and sheer volume of activity and travel I have coming up in the near future.

And this all plays out on me living in limbo at the moment.

I sold my home about a month ago and haven't quite figured out exactly where I'm going to live next. I have more money in the bank than I've ever had—by a lot—but for the moment I'm essentially homeless.

I don't like having so many events and planned activities on my calendar, and I don't like travel that takes me too far away from my family and those in my care.

Bob has me take my anxious parts to the same small secluded pond on our property that I had taken my Critic/Protector Parts to a few sessions ago.

I sit around the campfire and am present with them.

A Manager/Agent/Taskmaster/Coach type Part dressed in black, with a brusk, hyper-masculine, big city energy stands up and warns me that I have too much scheduled and that it's going to get in the way of my writing and creative and family time.

Another more gentle and feminine part moves over between me and him and begins to tell him he needs to relax and chill out. In many ways, these parts are the yin and yang of each other, the masculine and feminine, the push and pull of driving/getting things done versus relaxing/enjoying/flowing approaches.

When Bob has me ask the Agent/Manger Part how he sees me, he says it is as a young just-starting-out novelist in the early stages of learning/figuring out how to write a novel.

When I show him who I am now, he is blown away—not only by my age and experience, but my mastery of my craft and the size of my catalog. He is shocked and amazed at the number of books I've written and published.

He realizes that he's always been pushing me so hard to move to and work on the next book, that he hasn't stopped to enjoy and appreciate each accomplishment along the way.

In the light of seeing who I actually am and the work I've done, and in the presence of Self energy, he experiences a real paradigm shift. He becomes calm and settled and content.

He'll continue his job, but with a real change of energy and approach. He'll manage and support, but not demand and push relentlessly without enjoying the journey and relaxing along the way.

He does feel the need to remind me that his role is important and that I wouldn't have accomplished what I have if not for him, that a self-employed, self-starter, creative needs discipline and pushing.

The other part, the yin to his yang, remind him that it's okay if I never write another book or accomplish anything else, that it would be just fine if I took the summer off.

Sure the Manager/Pushy/Yang Part says, but reminder her I would be far less fulfilled.

They're both right.

I enjoy writing and creating. It's my way of being in the world. But I want to enjoy the process, the journey, and even embrace those aspects of life that interrupt and disrupt.

I realize that it's not so much all the events and activities and travel I have coming up, but my resistance to them that is causing me stress and discomfort.

Like my granddaughter resisting her nap, I am resisting that which is inevitable and good for me.

Bob say to let my various parts feel my calm energy and heart.

I do.

And as I do, I picture my sleeping granddaughter lying on my chest, her comfortable, peaceful, and deep sleep helped and aided by her heart beating next to her Grandu's beating heart below her.

INSIGHTS

In this session parts of me were resisting a change in routine, in travel, in schedule.

In studying resistance over the years, I've learned that we all have it—and that it is hardwired into us.

When we resist, the right side of the prefrontal region of our brains light up. This same region lights up when we experience negative emotions.

We experience resistance in the form of stress, anxiety, procrastination, denial, distraction, etc. anytime we're confronted with change or challenge or something we believe will be uncomfortable.

Like a horror movie where the call is coming from inside the house, that which is holding us, blocking us, preventing us from the new, the different, the other, is within us.

Rumi said that our job is not to seek for love, but to seek and find all the barriers to love we have built inside us.

I'd say our job is also to seek and find all the resistance in us, become aware of it, befriend it, see it clearly, acknowledge the importance of its job in certain circumstances, but see the ways it's holding us back in others and release it from the ways it's preventing us from change and growth.

The *Tao Te Ching* concept of Wu Wei is living without resistance. Wu Wei, or actionless action or effortless effort, says there's a great flow of life, like a river, and we do ourselves a disservice when we resist it or fight against it. In stead of swimming against the stream we should swim with it, which brings peace and balance and harmony and a flow that carries our actions along to an extent that they seem actionless.

Resistance blocks the flow of my life. My job is to seek and find those blockages, the parts of me that believe it's their job to resist and free them of that burden, so I can flow with the great river of life.

BOB'S NOTES

There is a support program called "Recovery International." It was originally called "Recovery Incorporated" when it was started in the 1930s by Abraham Low, a neurosychiatrist from Chicago. He wanted to help his patients support each other while also helping themselves use (and ultimately internalize) the objective language he used to help them "spot" what he called their "angry and fearful temper" so they could come to manage their "symptoms" and come to live healthier lives.

It is a cognitive behavioral approach with a group/communal support network to reinforce itself, well ahead of its time.

I find the language of Dr. Low has a wisdom that carries Self Energy. It has all the C's of Self (clarity, compassion, confidence, courage, creative, connected, calm, and curiousity).

One of my favorite "spots" came to mind as I read Michael's reflections. It is "to know is not to know."

Usually the harder my Parts try to do their job as they see it, the more blended I become. One of my most dominant Managers is the Need to Know. It will hold on until it passes out just like Michael's granddaughter.

But when I whisper to it with Self energy that "it's okay not to know"…and actually "to know is not to know" it loosens its grip and rests. It is free.

SESSION FOURTEEN

A pleasant early summer day, cool beneath a clear blue sky.

A small secluded garden, fragrant in verdant bloom, inside a larger wood.

Though it's not, or maybe it is, it seems a bit like the plush center of a huge hedge maze.

A little boy, alone, taking it all in.

Odd and out of place, and all the more significant for that, a full-size phone booth, the only non-organic object present.

My session with Bob today centers around a certain unsettledness.

I'm still in the season of change and transition, still without a home, still unsure exactly what and where my next home will be.

So many unknowns, so much up in the air, unsettled.

Part of me embraces the ambivalence and ambiguity, believing that knowing and control are illusions and too much settledness is a trap. My spiritual journey, the limits logic and understanding, and the impermanence of life has taught me that.

This part of me believes that the world was created out of

chaos and the chaos is still present, part of the very fabric of the cosmos.

But another part of me, a Little Boy Part, is activated and made anxious by uncertainty and unsettledness.

When I do a body scan and get curious, he is present.

He expresses that he doesn't like things not being settled. It makes him uncomfortable. He's accustomed to having a home —the same home—and the stability and security it provides. He says he's not afraid and even knows that it will all work out, but he's ready for that to happen. He wants that to happen now, wants out of limbo and back into being settled.

Another part, an older, settled and confident part, tells him to trust the process, to let things unfold, to breathe and be calm, trusting that everything will work out.

The Little Boy Part responds that he knows it will work out, but that he's just ready for it to.

Other parts appear and attempt to placate the Little Boy— an Older Brother Part, a Mother, and a Father.

They attempt to reassure the Little Boy, to comfort him.

Additionally, they try to figure out a way to short circuit the process, wanting to alleviate all his discomfort and dis-ease.

The older, wiser part reminds them this is not the way, that there is benefit and opportunity in this experience, to be with the Little Boy, but let him experience uncertainty and ambiguity and the open-endedness of existence.

The Little Boy Part is in a secluded garden in a wooded area.

There's a phone booth nearby.

Bob has me go to the Little Boy Part and introduced myself.

I do.

He thought he was me, didn't know he was a part.

I see that he is near the phone booth because he's calling for help.

When he sees me, he says "Dude, you're old."

I tell him that I am proof that he can trust the unfolding, that everything works out in profound and beautiful ways.

He sees that Self trusts the unfolding, and he and the other parts, who earlier wanted to end the process because of the anxiety it produced in the Little Boy, began to relax and become calm in the presence of Self.

"You can embrace and relax into unknowing and the unfolding—I'm the proof of that. Every part of life embraced and allowed to unfold becomes an incredible work of art. Every time. Trust. Relax. Embrace. Let go."

Self is home. Self is safe. Self is trustworthy. Remain calm and trust, soak up the calm, confident, compassionate energy of Self.

The Little Boy says that I am who he was waiting for to step out of the phone booth.

Bob says Clark Kent goes in and Super Man comes out.

To me Clark Kent is a part and Super Man is Self.

INSIGHTS

What is home?

Some definitions of home include: the place where one lives permanently, especially as a member of a family or household; relating to the place where one lives; (of a sports game) played at the team's own field or court; to or at the place where one lives; and (of an animal) return by instinct to its territory after leaving it.

I've spent the vast majority of my life (some 50 years) in the same small town. I've lived the vast majority of my life (some 45 years) in two houses, the one my parents raised me in and then the one I raised my children in, about 100 yards from each other.

Recently, I sold the second of these two homes, the one I had lived in for over 25 years, and moved out of what has been my neighborhood for 45 years.

Selling my home before I built or bought another one left me temporarily, literally, if not actually, homeless.

As you can imagine, this has led me to explore what home is and what it means.

And what I have realized more than anything else, what I

have experienced in the most profound way, is that I am my home.

Wherever I go, wherever I am, I'm home.
I'm home. I am home. I am my home.
Like a turtle, I carry my home with me.
What is home? I am. Where is home? Wherever I am.

BOB'S NOTES

Michael's phone booth metaphor is a perfect fit for IFS. It embodies some of the core queries that an IFS therapist might employ as he's working with a client to nurture curiosity.

Who is there?
How old are they?
Where are they right now?
Who do they think you are?
What is their purpose?

It also implies that there is a space between the caller and receiver. They are inherently unblended.

In the process other Parts might try to get on the phone and take over. But that's okay.

Are they willing to step back?
Do they need to be heard from first?

The IFS therapist might say, "I want everyone to know that I want to hear what they have to say...They are all important... They all belong."

Belonging is such a core need. All of our Parts have it...even when, like rebellious a teenager, they don't want to admit it.

It's okay to believe what you believe. It's okay to want what you want. It's okay to love who you love. It's okay to be as you are.

There's a beautiful song by Imagine Dragons called "It's okay not to be okay." It tells us that it's even okay NOT to be okay.

You still belong. No matter what.

SESSION FIFTEEN

A nondescript hotel bar.
Class reunion karaoke.
A tilting homemade banner that reads: WELCOME HOME WILDCATS.
Twenty years since graduation. Where has the time gone?
He rises from the table where he's sitting with his wife and a few close friends and their wives, and makes his way over to the bar.
It's his round.
At the bar while waiting his turn to order, he encounters another classmate sitting alone, knocking back Singapore Slings.
"Hey, man," he says. "How are you?"
He's not slurring his words quite yet but there's a slow, thick-tongued quality to his speech.
"Can you believe it's been twenty years?"
"I can't."
"I read part of that book you wrote."
"Oh, yeah? Which part?"

"Well... if I'm bein' honest... the part where they tell you about it on Amazon."

He laughs. "I'm sure there are those who'd say that's the best part."

"You... Looks like you're doin' some stuff... books and... that other stuff... but I gotta say. I thought you'd do more. Be... more... I don't know... successful or something. We all did."

"Yeah," he says with a sardonic expression and a heavy sigh, "me too."

Today I tell Bob I'd like to get curious about those parts of me that are never satisfied and are always wanting more.

I've been examining and interacting with these parts for a long time—long, long before I conceived of them as parts.

It's interesting. There are parts of me that aren't satisfied—not with where I am in my development as a human being, as a novelist, as a speaker/teacher, as a singer-songwriter, as a father, son, brother, friend, partner. These parts push me to be and do more. But only so far. I'm continually working on improving, but I'm not relentlessly, obsessively driven in the way many of the most outwardly seemingly successful among us are. I've often joked that my childhood was too happy and trauma free for that.

Parts of me are extremely happy and fulfilled and content. Other parts of me define success as that which is happening inside instead of outside of me.

But for today, I'm curious about those parts of me that aren't satisfied with the outward signs of success I have no control over—particularly as it relates to the general size of my readership and audience.

One of these parts is like a buddy in a bar at a class reunion, who wistfully and with no malice says, "I really thought you'd do more. Be more."

It's less a criticism than a resigned recognition, a forlorn and melancholic mood.

It's the frustration of an expectation. Of great expectations. The distance between the dream and the reality.

These parts are acutely aware of the ticking clock, of the brevity of life and soon certainly of death.

My arms bear these truths in black ink.

Momento Mori—Remember you will die and *Ultima Forsan*—perhaps this moment will be your last.

Every hour wounds and the last kills.

These parts are aware that time is running out.

They say do more now while you can, but they also lament the outcome of what has been done.

Another part steps forward and says that none of these things matter, that they're out of my control, and that I'm doing what matters most—caring for and enjoying family and friends, developing my gifts, following my passions, spreading love, creating, doing work that matters.

This part reminds the other parts to let go of any attachment to outcomes and love and embrace the process, the living, the doing, to *Amor fati*—love my fate.

There's a back and forth to this chorus of voices, the yin and yang pull of parts counter balancing each other.

One says that it's my expectations that are the primary culprit of my dissatisfaction.

One warns against longing, desire, and ambition, while another says they are vital for accomplishing and growing and evolving.

Other Peacemaker Parts argue for the need for balance, and not to be dominated by either, but especially not to live with a sense of dissatisfaction.

Another part says that the parts that are never satisfied are thieves that rob me of any sense of the joy of accomplishment because they're already driving toward the next task, next creation, next thing. They take me out of the present, steal that moment.

These parts see me as needing their input and motivation. Some of them see me as a young, unmotivated time-waster. Others see me as older with not much time left and lament all I haven't done.

Showing them who I actually am causes them to begin to reconsider, reconfigure their thinking.

In the presence of Self all these parts fall silent, relax, and let go of the burdens, the beliefs they carry, the weight of responsibility and expectation they labor beneath.

In the calm, confident, compassionate energy of Self there is need for nothing. There is peace. There is presence. Nothing is lacking. Nothing is done or undone or in need of doing.

Lao Tzu said, "When you realize nothing is lacking, the whole world belongs to you."

As Matsuo Basho wrote:

An old silent pond...
A frog jumps into the pond,
splash! Silence again.

INSIGHTS

"Trying to understand is like straining through muddy water. Have the patience to wait! Be still and allow the mud to settle. Do you have the patience to wait until your mud settles and the water is clear?" — Lao Tzu, *Tao Te Ching*

Parts have their place, and it's an important one. The jobs they do can be so helpful, but it's easy for them to get overly-activated. It's easy for them to believe that they must be extreme in their beliefs and duties.

And then . . . they become aware of Self, are bathed in the calm, confident, compassionate glow of Self.

"Stop thinking, and end your problems.
What difference between yes and no?
What difference between success and failure?
Must you value what others value,
avoid what others avoid?
How ridiculous!" — Lao Tzu, *Tao Te Ching*

All my activated parts take on too much responsibility and fail to trust—fail to trust me, life, the universe.

They attempt to control outcomes rather than trust and allow the unfolding.

The price for this is my joy and peace, satisfaction and serenity.

Self is pure, is peaceful, is complete.

I am content.

I am overwhelmed with gratitude, so happy and grateful to be here.

BOB'S NOTES

We got two new kittens the other day. It's the beginning of my kid's summer break and the best time to get a new animal. In my family the general rule is, "Whatever animal Dad allows" will soon be part of the household. I had planned on getting only one, but when another wanted to sit in my son's lap the whole time, I was sold. We are up to 6 cats, 2 dogs, and one bearded dragon (a reptile who's about 20 inches from nose to tail).

This time, I think the kittens were just as much for me and for everybody else. They bring me right to the present.

I was meeting today with a couple in their early 20s. We were getting curious about how what we are exposed to creates our reality. I was reflecting on the kittens and how their entire world is my son's bedroom. It is safe. It is their new womb.

I was telling the couple how exciting it is to watch the kittens when we open the door and they begin exploring down the hall. I can almost feel the energy inside their little bodies. They are so curious. Through their eyes I experience life fresh and anew.

I return to the couple who have each described their understanding of depression. They share their experiences and their fears. We get curious. They are receptive to hold what they know loosely. Together we "begin exploring down the hall."

Consider allowing yourself to find a hallway inside of you that you are curious about. Notice what Parts arise in response to the hallway. Let yourself slow down. There's no need to get beyond what is in front of you. Just sit with it and breathe. You might place your hand on your heart or your stomach to feel the response of your body, and also allow your body to feel your physical presence.

This is enough. You are enough.

SESSION SIXTEEN

"The mind of the beginner is empty, free of the habits of the expert, ready to accept, to doubt, and open to all the possibilities." —Shunryu Suzuki

This week's session is unique.

I'll be giving an inspirational talk at the Unitarian Universalist Church this weekend and ask Bob if we can do parts work related to my topic.

I've chosen for my topic embracing not knowing, uncertainty, and living with beginners mind, so I'd like to get curious about and explore the parts of me that are uncomfortable with uncertainty and those parts of me that are comfortable with it.

In the context of the talk, Bob mentioned all the cool things and great opportunities I have going, and all the way I connect with people and connect them with each other through music, books, and inspirational talks.

It reminded me of what one of the organizers and movers and shakers in the art community said to me recently—that I was a connector of people.

As we get curious . . .

I have a Young Professor Part who resides in my head.

He's a seeker with a real thirst for truth, knowledge, wisdom, and experience.

A student and a teacher, he is an academic, an intellectual, and his job is to seek for answers.

He sees me as a young man about his age.

Another part, a Heart Part joins us. Located in my chest, this Self-like part warns of the limitations of reason, logic, and knowledge. He believes there's a real futility to knowledge, and sees the incompleteness in all answers. He tells the Seeker Part that he can't really know much of anything, and encourages him to practice not knowing and beginners mind.

The Seeker believes the Heart Part is just saying this because he's old and complacent and lazy and not willing to seek.

When I introduce my Self to these parts, the Seeker not only sees that I am older and wiser and completely fine with being curious and not knowing, but that I still share his youthful exuberance for seeking and searching and learning.

The Heart Part says it's okay to seek, but not to trust in the illusion of the certainty of answers nor cling to knowing, knowledge, or answers.

The Seeker is happy to hear him say this. He realizes that he can do his job of seeking and bring information with freedom. He no longer has to work under the pressure of knowing and finding answers. He sees that he can actually seek for and gather information and knowledge without the responsibility for having to do anything with it.

Self takes the Professor/Seeker Part to a secret library that contains all the books of the world—all the wisdom, all the knowledge, and he basks in the mystery of knowledge and not knowing with no no pressure or clinging. It's both magic and liberating.

Even as this is happening another part in my lower abdomen expresses discomfort with not knowing, but seems to let go of the burden of it, at least for the moment, by just saying it.

INSIGHTS

The power of IFS is in the practice of it, the fact that it engages both mind and body, that it is intellectual, imaginative, and somatic.

Unlike other therapies that engage only aspects of who we are, IFS engages every part and all parts of us.

It's experiential.

It takes that which could be purely mental or emotional and incarnates it, allows us to experience it in profound and meaningful ways.

Before this session I could've told you that I have an Intellectual/Professor/Seeker Part and an Intuitive/Heart Part, but this awareness and knowledge can only take me so far. Through IFS parts work I got to experience these parts, to interact with, to engage with, to have an actual experiential Self-led internal session, reaching levels and depths mere awareness or talking about these things could never provide.

It's the difference of about 18 inches—roughly the distance from my head to my heart, from mind to body, from mere knowledge to actual lived experience.

I am too often in my head, out of balance in my top down approach. IFS parts work, beginning with a body scan, allows for a more bottom up approach that connects and rebalances head and heart, mind and body, and gives me a rich, integrated experience of both.

BOB'S NOTES

Living primarily in an unblended space is a wonderful thing. Michael just described it as balanced and integrated. When I've been living in a tornado of blended Protectors, it feels like Grace.

I came to therapy as a young man believing he had lost THE Love of his life. It took a few years for me to even begin considering dating. The Stay away and Freeze Protectors were keeping me safe.

As the prospect of dating became a topic in my sessions with Marshall, he would periodically remind me, "Bob, it takes 100." I didn't like this at all. I didn't want to have to go through the process. I didn't want to let go. I didn't trust I'd be "caught."

No! Stop! Don't!

Intellectually I knew another person couldn't "catch" me. I had doubts I could catch myself and the jury was out on whether there was any kind of "higher power" that would catch me.

Figure it out...Doubt...Caution.

I was reluctant to trust. I wasn't like those kittens from the previous session. My Protectors were leading the way.

Never stop checking for your parachute...Brace for Impact......Be careful...

These Protectors are still a part of my life. They are usually softer and less compelled to blend, but it still happens.

This is a process. "It takes 100."

SESSION SEVENTEEN

Pickup basketball in the old red-brick gym on Main Street.

Antique hardwood court and wooden bleachers, old goals, echoes.

Bouncing ball smacking the floor, careening off the rim, slapping hands, swishing through the nets. Sneakers screeching on the court. Grunts. Groans. Yells. Laughs. Trash talk.

Ghosts of games past.

No air conditioning. No moving air. Stifling, sauna-like heat.

Random group.

Mostly young men half his age. Some teens nearly a quarter.

A couple of new players. Changed dynamic.

A soft, flabby guy with little ability and less skill takes a bad shot.

"Foul!" he yells.

"That wasn't a foul!" the defender says. "I didn't touch you. That was all ball."

"It was fuckin' foul. Give me the damn ball."

Slinging the ball at him, the defender says, "That's some bullshit. I didn't fuckin' touch you."

"Come on," the older guy says. "We don't argue fouls. If someone calls it that's what we go with. Let's stop arguing and play."

"Score?" one of the other players asks.

"12-7," the guy who missed the bad shot and called foul says.

"No way," his defender says. "Hell no. You're not gonna—It's 10-9."

theH older guy, who has been keeping the score and announcing it after every possession, says, "It's 12-11," he says.

"*12-11*? No fuckin' way."

"I've been keeping up with it," the older guy says. "I've said what it is after every made basket. That's the score."

"Who's way?"

"Ours."

"Bullshit. No way."

"That is the score," he says. "I wouldn't say it if I didn't know. But I didn't come out here to argue. I'm here to play ball. Y'all say what the score is and we'll go with that."

"It's 12-7."

"No, it's 10-9."

"Guys, come on."

Their core group never has these issues. They play with respect and good sportsmanship. The two new guys are ruining the games.

8 guys standing around waiting while two guys argue.

His frustration is growing.

"That's not how we play here," he says. "We don't argue over calls or the score. We just play and we call our own fouls with no arguing."

"He fouled me and the score is 12-7."

"Okay, I'm done. I didn't come here to listen to y'all bicker and I certainly didn't come to argue with you."

As he gathers his things and walks out into the fresh air of evening, he doesn't just feel frustrated at the two guys who were constantly arguing, but at himself for letting it get to him. He's ashamed of his reaction and feels guilty for it.

In my session with Bob today, I share with him how a part of me got activated playing basketball at the gym last night, how I got frustrated with the tone of the competition and especially the bickering and arguing two of the guys were doing.

I shared with him how before the last game ended, I stopped playing, told them I didn't come to argue, and left.

I shared with him how part of me was disappointed in that response and regretted it.

With compassion and understanding he said how hot and tired and compromised I must have been after playing for an hour and a half in the heat at my age.

I told him how I did feel compromised and fatigued from the night before. After a long work day and playing a three hour gig , I had run some errands for my children and then driven a few hours to pick up one of my grandchildren and how I hadn't gotten much sleep. And how the heat and exertion only added to it.

We got curious and the part that came up immediately was a Young Boy Part who's very much my leader, competitor, organizer. He was the leader of the backyard ball of childhood and always felt like he was hurting cats as he tried to organize and keep games going.

He enjoyed competing and winning.

Another part joined him, an older Adolescent Part who had undergone a spiritual awakening and is more interested in spiritual and creative pursuits, and is almost anti-competition. He's gentle and kind and not as aggressive or asserting as the Little Boy Part.

I spend time with both parts, letting them see who I am now, and sharing Self energy with them. I validate them, reminding them how they're both necessary and how much I appreciate the job each of them do.

I take the Young Competitive Part to the empty gym and we hang out and that space changes somewhat for him—his experience of it and his approach to it.

Eventually the older, Adolescent/Spiritual Seeker/Creative Part joins us.

Both parts gain a new appreciation for each other, see each other more clearly, see me more clearly, and have their roles infused with Self energy.

A Perfectionist Part appears and says he is still disappointed that I got so frustrated and left last night. Also present but not very active or visible, sort of hanging out beneath these other parts is a part that practices the avoidance of conflict as much as possible. He'd prefer I not compete at all.

All parts benefit from time with Self in the old, empty gym, and experience a new freedom and joy—especially the Little Competitor Part.

INSIGHTS

Everything is my teacher.

When I am aware and open and teachable, I learn, I am transformed.

What will I learn today? Depends on how much of a student I am. And who I perceive as my teacher.

I want to be a student at all times—for when the student is ready, the teacher will come.

I want to be learning, growing, evolving, becoming—playing pick up basketball no less than meditating, playing with my grandchildren no less than studying the Tao Te Ching or reading Rumi.

Playing basketball is great exercise, good for both my mental and physical health, but how much better for me is it when I'm aware of which of my parts get triggered—why and by what?

BOB'S NOTES

The past is present.

This is an invaluable reminder for me as I'm connecting with my clients and their Parts. And sometimes there is more than one "past" that is "present" at the same time.

Michael's session today explored a few different parts living in different memories and times from the past. As he got curious and began unblending, it became possible for these Parts to coexist and actually become aware of each other.

Relationships in IFS have different forms. All of them contain important information.

Today's session with Michael reminded me that Parts can have reactions to each other.

One of the starting points for getting curious about a Part is the therapist asking, "How do you feel towards this Part." If the answer doesn't contain Self energy (one of the 8 Cs), then it's another Part who is responding to the question.

Then we ask the second Part if it is willing to give some space so we can connect with the first part. If the second part needs to be heard from, then we ask the first part to give some space and let it know we won't forget about it.

This can take some negotiation. Sometimes they both want to be heard from at the same time.

A helpful exercise I was taught was to ask my client to gently hold one of the parts in her left hand and the other in her right. I'll have her spend a little time focusing on the Part held in each hand, noticing that there is space between them. We'll engage with each Part as the other Part "observes." No part is ignored. Each part is valued.

Often they will gradually unblend.

You might find two parts within you that are present as you are reading this. Give each of them one of your hands. What do you notice?

SESSION EIGHTEEN

"Are you okay?" he asks.

He senses a small, subtle change in her, the slightest shift in her mood.

"Why do you ask?" she says.

"Just thought I sensed something was wrong."

"I'm okay. Not sure what it is . . . guess I feel a little off. Can't believe you even noticed."

"Anything I can do for you?" he asks.

She shakes her head. "Not that I can think of."

He starts to ask if she's sure and to offer some things he could do for her, but stops.

Pause.

Part of him wants to press the issue, figure out a way he can help her. This part is convinced he can help her if she'll let him.

Another part of him is learning to let go—to care, to check on, to offer support, but not to try to fix or take responsibility for.

Which part will win? Will he give into old, ingrained habits of emotional heroism or will he step back, let go, practicing non-attachment in love? And what would he have done if this has been a more extreme issue instead of something so small?

In my session with Bob today we spent a lot of time talking about how good everything is and how grateful I am.

My children and parents, family and friends, are happy and healthy. My work is going well.

Life is so rich and sweet and full.

I've recently started seeing someone who I've known for thirty years. We are moving extremely slow, with great care and thought and caution, and trusting the gradual unfolding.

This slow approach and the accompanying autonomy we're each maintaining is far different from earlier relationships where I've impatiently rushed the process, projected onto the other person qualities, traits, and characteristics that weren't there and overlooked the flapping red flags that were. In the past, instead of allowing for a slow unfolding or walking away sooner, I have too quickly taken too much responsibility for the other person and the relationship itself, attempting to heal and help them and make the relationship work, instead of asking if it should.

Not so now. And never again.

When I get curious and conduct a body scan, I feel a warm, intense heart energy.

This Heart Part is so grateful, so content.

I become aware that this part is most often happy and peaceful when all my family and friends and loved ones are good and in a good place. And when they're not how it works to help them to get me back to a place of peace, love, and joy.

This Heart Part with Self-energy is a helper and healer and lover with a big heart and a big issue—his serenity and contentedness and joy is contingent on his loved ones being happy. This is especially true of my children, but applies to varying degrees to everyone in my orbit.

Bob has me ask the part how he sees me. It sees me as a

young boy who believes his peace and joy are found in helping others experience those same things, and who is far too sensitive to outward conditions and situations, particularly the relative state of others.

Seeing me as I am now, experiencing Self, he sees that his happiness, joy, fulfillment, and peace is not contingent on that of others, that it is not his job to fix anything or make others better.

His burden has been the belief that he's responsible for others, that it was his job to help make them happy, and that his happiness was directly connected if not completely contingent on theirs. This belief and the practice of its burden emanated out of him in concentric circles, flowing firstly and mostly to those who are closest and for whom he feels the most responsibly.

His job has been to make others happy, and his relative happiness has been too tied to theirs.

As he's seeing that he can care for others and do what he can for them, even taking steps toward aiding in their happiness and fulfillment, without taking responsibility for them, a Critic Part tells him that caring about or doing any less for others is selfish and self-centered.

"How can you be truly happy when others aren't? How can you be compassionate if you're not feeling what they feel?"

Another part says that actually trying to make someone happy so you can be happy is in part a selfish act.

This leads to a back and forth and some attempts at convincing each other among the parts.

"It's not selfish or self-centered to care for yourself. You aren't responsible for others. Think about it. You wouldn't allow anyone to take responsibility for you."

"That's true."

"You've always been pretty good at self-care. You've just sometimes slipped into care-taking of others, taking responsibility for their happiness and allowed it to have too much impact on your own."

Bob looks back at his notes from my very first session, and recalls how I said I was there to address being too outwardly and others directed and to work on not letting compassion or caring cross the line into care-taking and taking responsibility for others, to stop being a fixer.

I told him I've seen growth in this area, how it had begun long before I began IFS, but how the parts work we've been doing has helped tremendously in the process. And how today's work gets at the heart of the matter. I feel free and unburdened.

INSIGHTS

It brings me more joy than I can say to share love with others. I feel like I'm fluent in the languages of love—acts of service, words of affirmation, quality time, physical touch, and giving gifts.

I love receiving these as well.

For me, true unconditional love is when these are given freely with no expectation and no attachment to response or outcome.

That's the goal I've been working toward all of my life, and as with any practice I've gotten better at it the more I've practiced it over the years.

When I am free and unburdened love flows from Self to me, all my parts, and others—without expectation or agenda.

However, when certain parts of me get activated, their beliefs hinder and block the free flow of love. They can expect a certain response or something in return. They can have an agenda, such as rescuing or taking responsibility for the other person and their happiness. They can even believe, falsely, of course, that someone is unworthy of love. All these are the barriers to love that Rumi said is my job to seek and remove.

"Your task is not to seek for love, but merely to seek and find all the barriers within yourself that you have built against it."
Parts work helps me with this process.

BOB'S NOTES

As I was reading Michael's reflections on this session, the movie "The Princess Bride" came to mind. In its own farcical and tender way, it leads us to consider what is "true love?"

Princess Buttercup's actual "true love" Wesley continually professes his love for her saying "As you wish." At another point, Princess Buttercup is being forced to marry "the bad guy." The priest performing the ceremony has this ridiculously pronounced lisp. He intends to say "Love, true love..." but what comes out "Wub twu wub." It's both hilarious and poignant.

There is a 12 Step Program called "Sex and Love Addicts Anonymous" (SLAA). Fundamentally it is a place for people challenged with navigating boundaries (physical or emotional) in relationship to others and within themselves.

There are other 12 Step programs whose focus is primarily on the sexual behavior. They include Sex Addicts Anonymous (SAA), Sexaholics Anonymous (SA), and Sexual Compulsives Anonymous (SCA). SLAA also encompasses the emotional entanglements, projection and trauma responses.

In Alcoholics Anonymous the 1st step is "Admitted we were powerless over alcohol-that our lives had become unmanageable." The 2nd step is "Came to believe that a power greater than ourselves could restore us to sanity." In SLAA, the powerlessness is related to how "addiction" manifests in intimate relationships. One cautionary reminder is, "Don't make another person your 'higher power'."

We are so often given the messages that:

1. Some other person whom we come to "love" will make us happy.

2. We are responsible for making the person we "love" happy.

Years ago, my wife and I were working through some of our own issues and she came across this quote, "I love my false image of you." I've returned to this valuable reminder over and over again.

Am I really seeing the other person? Do I only "love" the ideal that I project upon them? How do I get clarity about this? What "Parts" are taking over and blending?

What is love?

For more information check out the websites for any of the above listed 12 Step programs where meetings (virtual and in person) are posted as well. I also recommend anything written by Patrick Carnes.

SESSION NINETEEN

An old, wooden desk sits in his library.

A simple, single person office desk, dark and unremarkable.

Marred, nicked, splintered in spots, the single drawer in the center catches as it clunkily slides in and out, wood scraping wood.

Part of an old sticker with emergency contacts on it for Fire, Police, and Ambulance that pre-dates 911 slants down at an odd angle on the front right side.

He loves and cherishes the old desk, every grain of the wood, every scar, loves having it in his library/study, surrounded by his old books.

He's the fourth generation of his family to sit at it, to do his work on it.

In his family's small-town hardware store, his father sat at it before him, and his father before him, and his father before him.

It's priceless to him, this old, simple, piece of office furniture that wasn't expensive or nice when it was new, remarkable in its unremarkableness, a legacy, an heirloom.

Sitting the old desk in my study, meeting virtually with Bob, we talk about the possibility of me training in IFS to add to my pastoral counseling and life coaching. As usual, Bob is very helpful, supportive, and encouraging.

When we transition from talking to parts work, we get curious about a deep part of me that can be shy and self-conscious, particularly about performing—a part that is sensitive to criticism, comparison, or and judgment.

I've heard of a lover being described as a kind of shy child. This part reminds me of that.

Three parts surface simultaneously.

One close to my heart and two just below my heart.

The Heart Part is a little boy, sensitive and shy, easily embarrassed.

The other parts—the ones in my abdomen—are a Teenage Part and a Father Figure Part, both of whom are protective of the Little Boy Part and want to keep him safe from pain and embarrassment.

The Little Boy part doesn't like attention and gets embarrassed easily.

Bob had me let the Little Boy Part see me as I am now.

He was surprised at my age. And noticed immediately how strong, calm, and peaceful I am. He sees that I rarely get self-conscious or shy and don't embarrass easily.

When asks what he wants, the Little Boy Part says he wants to be free to play without any self-consciousness and without the input and protection of any Protector Parts.

Another part comes forward then, my Fearless Artist Part, and tells the Boy Part that he doesn't need to be afraid or embarrassed or ashamed, and that he doesn't need to listen to anyone. Just needs to do his own thing, freely and openly, with joy and abandon.

The Father Figure Part is overly protective—not unlike my dad when I was young and me to a lesser degree as a young dad.

I think about my dad's childhood, how it shaped and formed him, how responsive and protective it made him, and how, unsurprisingly, my internal Dad Part has many similar characteristics and traits.

Bob wonders if aspects of this have a legacy dimension to them.

I question and reflect and determine there is an Overly Protective Legacy Part present.

Bob explains the process involved in releasing a Legacy Part into a talisman, in having the part come out of me and go into something else.

He says by choosing a befitting object the part can be outside of but still connected to me—and still close enough to check in with if need be.

I think about it, ponder on the process.

I really like the idea that connection can be maintained but with space and boundaries and without the voice inside me.

Bob mentions a few possible objects I might use, but I immediately know what it should be—the very desk I'm sitting at, touch at the moment, the desk that had been my dad's and his dad's in our family's hardware store.

I release the part and invite it to reside in the desk.

I am overwhelmed with gratitude, with appreciation for all the protection—a protection that flows out of love and care and concern.

Tears begin to flow.

I think of all the children who didn't receive adequate or much of any protection at all and I'm so grateful and feel so loved and cared for—even or especially when the protection was veered into extreme caution and over protection.

Bob suggests a possible exercise for this week might be to spend time imagining that Father Figure Part receiving everything he needed when he was a Little Boy Part and the difference that would make in his life and mine.

INSIGHTS

My home, which is where I both live and work, is filled with objects that are sacred to me.

This makes my home a sanctuary.

There are my books, of course—thousands of them—each a portable magic, a portal to another dimension.

Antique typewriters.

My guitars.

My incense and incense burners.

My art and art books.

My alter.

My film memorabilia.

The photographs of my family.

The drawings and art projects created by my grandchildren.

Religious statues and iconography.

My book awards.

Gifts given to me by my family and friends.

The single board from the dining room door frame in my old house that charts the growth of my children with pencil marks.

And, of course, the old wooden desk from my family's old hardware store, which means even more now that it has become a legacy talisman.

BOB'S NOTES

What is mine? What isn't mine?

IFS allows us to explore Parts of us both subjectively and objectively. One of questions we might ask of a Part is, "How old are you?" Sometimes the answer is clear. A vivid memory or felt experience. Sometimes is nebulous. I find that often, when it is unclear, the Part may be something that is older than us. A Legacy.

Some Legacies carry a sense of belonging. Some can carry beliefs of deep shame.

I have found that connecting with Legacy's can provide relief and freedom as well as a deeper sense of connection and empathy for those who came before us.

We are all standing on somebody else's shoulders.

Consider a Part of you that resonates with one of your parents or ancestors. It can be a Part you "like" or one that is challenging. Invite that Part to sit in front of you, giving you just enough space so you are aware it is separate from you. Ask the Part to become aware of you. Stay curious about what stories it might have to tell. Thank it for anything it shares and its willingness to trust you.

SESSION TWENTY

Can't sleep. No matter how hard I try.
    Don't feel like myself.
    Heart rate elevated.
    Not one. Not two. But three migraines in less than a week.
    Dark thoughts. Guilt and shame. Regrets. Heightened sense of the ticking clock of mortality.
    What's going on? This isn't like me at all. So rare that I feel anything like this. What's causing it?
    It has to be the medicine. A bad reaction to it.
    I rarely take medication of any kind. And side effects like these are part of the reason.
    Earlier in the week, a walk-in clinic doctor gave me a steroid for a skin irritation I had which he called dermatitis.
    I discontinue the steroid immediately.
    In my session with Bob this week, I shared with him my experience with the steroid I was taking for my dermatitis, the terrible way it made me fee and the dark place it took me to—mostly in terms of regrets and my mortality.
    When we begin parts work by getting curious, a masculine

Coach Part who is always encouraging me to push myself to do more, to accomplish more, came forward.

Bob asks when this part first appeared and I said when I was in college in Atlanta. It was then that I first recall him judging and criticizing me for what I did with my free time. When I would watch a movie or chill out, this part would tell me I needed to be doing something else—reading, meditating, developing my talents, going out and taking advantage of the incredible city I was living in. But this same part had been present much longer in different ways.

A Female Teacher Part with some maternal traits is activated and attempts to protect me from the Coach Part. She tells him I'm doing plenty and that my heart is amazing. She says I am enough and I'm doing enough.

There's a real yin and yang, back-and-forth, pull push pull between the two parts and both are coming from a good place, believing they are doing what is best for me.

Bob has me share with the parts who I am now.

They see that I'm not a little boy or a teenager in college, but a grown man in his fifties—calm, confident, compassionate, creative.

A transformation takes place, a shift of insight and understanding in the two activated parts.

The Coach Part acknowledges that what matters most is who I am far more than what I do. He doesn't want to stop doing his job, just make some modifications and alterations order to take a different approach.

There's a good energy and flow between the two parts, a harmony to their yin and yang flow.

But even as this good flow is happening, a six-year-old Little Boy Part residing deep within my lower abdomen comes forward and expresses his strong desire for everyone to get along.

Bob has me take him somewhere else, and I take him to the

top of a high hill in Fort Knox, Kentucky, where I visited once as a child.

The Little Boy Part feels relaxed and calm and safe.

Bob asks if there's a difference between wanting everybody happy and feeling responsible for their happiness.

The Little Boy Part realizes immediately that there is and begins to feel free—the freedom that comes from the release of responsibility for other's happiness. A happiness and joy infuse the Little Boy Part as the unburdening takes place. He wants everyone to experience this freedom and happiness, but he no longer feels responsible for ensuring they do.

INSIGHTS

Since my factory default settings are mostly positive and hopeful, I tend to look closely at when and why I feel in ways that contradict them.

When I feel less positive or hopeful I often ask myself if it is actually more accurate than when I'm feeling my usual positivity and hopefulness.

I rarely take medication of any kind. In many cases I feel like the so called cure is far worse than the ailment it's meant to address. That was certainly the case with the steroid I was prescribed to treat my dermatitis.

And yet, even when I'm fairly certain that the way I'm feeling is directly connected to medication I'm taking (or fatigue or lack of sleep or hunger), I still attempt to examine it to see if it's more accurate or can at least provide additional insights.

This is what I was doing leading up to this session.

And I'm always surprised and often fascinated by the parts that come forward during parts work, where they're located, and what they believe. It's rarely as direct or straightforward as

I believe it's going to be based on what I enter the session wanting to explore.

BOB'S NOTES

My Part that feels "responsible for" others has been a dominant force in my life. I'm sure it had a significant impact on my choice of profession.

As long as I can remember I've felt responsible for other's feelings, especially towards me. A first step towards clarity came when Marshall explained the difference between being responsible FOR someone and being responsible TO someone.

He said we are ONLY responsible FOR ourselves and our children while they are growing up. We are responsible TO our parents, friends, coworkers, society and the earth.

Being mindful of how our choices and behavior impact others demonstrates responsibility. That awareness combined with intentionality fosters characteristics like respect and dignity. We create more space for the 8 Cs of Self energy.

The first agreement in Don Miguel Ruiz' book "The Four Agreements" is, "Be impeccable with your word." He explains how words are like magic. They can have immense power and impact, so we must be aware of how we are using them.

What's even more important than how I use my words

(power) with others, is how I use them with myself. Words create beliefs. Parts hold these beliefs. Beliefs can be burdens.

When we get curious about Parts and the beliefs they carry, we can begin to deconstruct them. As we deconstruct them we come to understand what they represent to that Part. As the Part becomes aware of this, it experiences its own sense of freedom. It has a choice about what words it uses and what those words actually mean to it.

SESSION TWENTY-ONE

He's spent their entire lives protecting them.

Before he is anything else—a son, a brother, a friend, a husband, a novelist, a teacher—he's a father. It's his defining characteristic.

In the hospital when they were born, while also caring for their mom as she recovered from a C-section, he held them and cared for them and refused to leave them. And moments after the neonatal nurses wheeled them down to the nursery he headed down to wheel them right back to their room.

Throughout their lives he's cared for and provided for and protected them—attempting as much as possible to identify and prevent even potential dangers long before they had the slightest possibility of happening.

It's his number one most important job—and he has a strong work ethic. It's his number one responsibility—and he's known for being overly responsible.

He will be their dad, be available to them, love and support them, their entire lives—well, for the rest of his—but their childhoods are over and they will likely need him less and less.

He's done his most important job—delivered them to adulthood safe and happy and healthy, and without myriad unknown traumas and scars they might have had if he hadn't been their dad, hadn't approached that great honor in the manner he did.

He's done all this and done it well—until this moment.

Now he's about to undo some of it. How much he can't be sure, but far, far more than he ever thought he would.

He, along with his wife, their mother, are about to call their children in, sit them down, and tell them after over twenty-two years of marriage they're getting a divorce.

Bob and I begin by talking about my week.

I played a songwriters event last night and it went extremely well.

Much of my week has been getting ready and preparing for it—in and around and in between working on my latest novel, playing with my granddaughters, and spending time with my family and friends.

I love writing and sharing my songs.

I'm still very new at it—coming to it in midlife after thirty years of other forms of writing.

After a few years of learning to play guitar and sing by playing other artist's songs, I've been writing and playing my own, and it is an extremely rewarding experience. It's both different and similar to my other creative and artistic endeavors, and like them gives meaning and depth to my existence.

I share with Bob how happy and pleased I am with the entire experience and how different it is from my horrible experience with the steroid medication last week.

I felt so bad last week, got so down, and felt so much regret.

I share with him how I have very few big regrets.

I have lots and lots of little ones, but, gratefully, not many big ones at all.

I've largely lived a loving life on my own terms and mostly treated others with kindness and compassion. I've spent my life in self-development, spiritual practices, creative pursuits, and caring for others. And for the most part I've had the right priorities throughout—especially when it comes to my children and family and doing what matters most.

That being said, there's room for improvement in every area, and if I could go back I would certainly do things differently—but only if I had the knowledge and experience that I have now, which, of course, I wouldn't.

I believe that's why Maya Angelou admonishes us to "do the best you can until you know better. Then when you know better, do better."

I share with Bob how the single greatest regret of my life is putting my children through a divorce. I waited until they were grown or nearly grown, and moved slowly and carefully through the process while truly putting them first, even keeping our family under one roof for two years following the divorce, and though these are obviously mitigating factors, I still deeply regret it, still feel enormous guilt and shame.

Today, some thirteen years later I can detect no obvious wounds or negative impacts on my children, nor can I imagine how their mom and I could've handled things any better or more lovingly than we did, and yet I still feel regret, shame, and guilt.

Bob asks what I modeled for my children.

As honest and objective as I can be, I say I molded unconditional love for them. I truly put them first. I modeled love and respect for their mom. I gave them a safe, healthy family in a loving, stable, supportive environment.

I then share with him how this isn't just my perception or wishful thinking, but what they have said. I read for him two of the messages I received from them on Father's Day. One wrote, "You're the most loving and supportive dad ever, and I hope I can be just like you when I have kids." Another one wrote,

"You've given me unconditional love every minute of every day of my entire life. Love you so much."

Bob asks if part of what I modeled for them is that you don't have to stay stuck in a relationship or a situation.

I've never really considered this before.

He asks if my previous partner ever said or did anything to make me feel guilty or ashamed, and I told him absolutely not.

I told him how differently I feel about ending other relationships compared to the one that involved my children.

And even though I don't detect any adverse effects from the divorce on the kids and can't imagine a more amicable and loving process, part of me still feels such guilt, shame, and regret.

I realize that the part of me that feels guilt, shame, and regret, feels responsible.

As I get curious, a Young Father Part surfaces.

Like me at that age in life, he's not only a father to his young daughter, but a father to the children and youth in the parish where he serves. He's earnest and sensitive and feels things deeply. He's a true believer with a desire to be an example of love and compassion. He feels a high level of responsibility as a father and a minister, and has a perfectionistic part and a part that cares too much about how others perceive him.

He's on a genuine and authentic spiritual journey, and bears the burden of feeling responsible for others and caring too much about his perceived role as a representative of Christ and the church.

My interaction with this part is mingled with my memories of myself at that age.

Bob asks me to take him somewhere to show him who I am now and let him be in the presence of Self.

I take him to the sanctuary of the church I was serving—not on a Sunday or Wednesday when services were taking place, but on the weekday mornings when I would enter it alone to pray and meditate.

The large sanctuary is dark and quiet, a holy place made more holy by its emptiness.

We sit on the front pew together.

He sees who I am now—where the past thirty years of my journey have led me.

Bob asks me to take my parts to the place where I met with the youth of the church.

I have them join me upstairs in the educational building in the large youth room.

My Young Father/Minister Part in a sky-blue clerical collar is standing behind the podium, as if he's about to deliver a message, but Self asks him to take a seat with the other parts seated in the folding chairs.

All the parts see me as I am now. They sit together with the expectation that Self is going to deliver a message or teach them something.

But there are no words. Self is present and flowing from it is a powerful energy—calm, compassion, clarity confidence—flowing from Self to the different parts.

As this happens, the Young Father begins to release his sense of being responsible for everyone, bringing calm and clarity, and a new sense of freedom.

INSIGHTS

I am responsible for me.

I am not responsible for others.

I was responsible for my children when they were children.

I am responsible for my grandchildren when they're with me.

I have spent far too much of my life feeling and attempting to be overly-responsible, including for others and things they were responsible for.

When I take responsibility for others I diminish their agency and autonomy.

I am in the ongoing process of letting go of my belief that I'm responsible for others.

I am responsible for me.

I am not responsible for others.

But I am responsible to others.

I'm responsible for me. I'm accountable to others.

BOB'S NOTES

Each of us is a canvas. I don't paint or draw, but I can guide my clients in creating their own inner canvas. Using IFS I have become more confident in using my creativity and imagination.

Symbols, metaphors, and myths are gateways to discovering meaning in our lives. As a storyteller, Michael instinctually goes there.

I have one client who likes to draw and is drawn toward trees. In a session we began allowing her Parts to identify as different types of trees. Each had its own space but they were also all connected underneath the ground. This helped her unblend without the Parts feeling abandoned, while also honoring their unique qualities. She followed this on her own and a few sessions later she showed me the drawings she had made of the trees.

Another client is a retired and high school teacher and basketball coach. He resonates with Self as the classroom teacher and the coach in a practice. He is quick to access curiosity towards his Parts when he sees them as students or boys her coached.

I've been working with an octogenarian who has a passion

for large cats and still works with them. We frequently reflect on feline qualities of some of his Parts. When he engages with them the way he intuitively engages with cats, Self energy manifests.

I encourage you to find the world, passion, profession, or safe place that works for you. Invite your Parts to join you there.

SESSION TWENTY-TWO

Pulse pounding.
    Adrenaline spiking.
    Mercury rising into the red.
    He can feel it building inside of him.
    Pressure.
    Frustration.
    Then...
    Loss of control.
    Letting go.
    Explosion.

I share with Bob today how I periodically lose my temper, or lose control, or have an outburst of anger, how it often comes from frustration and usually happens when I am compromised physically, mentally, or emotionally—especially fatigued and sleep-deprived.

It's a truly rare occurrence, often with years in between, but it happened recently, and I'd like to explore it in the context of IFS and parts work.

While waiting to build my new home, I've been living in a RV camper on the property.

I'e been living in this small, cramped, confined space for going on four months.

Full-time for four months—months of bumping into the walls and furniture and knocking things over, taking showers in a tube that is too narrow to even bend over in.

I've found aspects of it frustrating, but it hasn't been too bad. I haven't been too bothered by it.

But last week, in the middle of the night, after having fallen asleep on the small loveseat, I was carrying several things to the bedroom to go to bed. I hadn't slept well the past few nights before, and I was carrying a glass of water, a book, my phone, headphones, and a few other items.

As I attempted to balance everything while moving the doorstop and closing the door with my foot, I spilled the glass of water and it went everywhere—on my phone, my book, the wall, the door, the floor.

In a moment of aggravation and frustration I threw everything else down to join the water and glass on the floor.

Bob suggests that the action I took has significance, that the action was to let everything go, to rid myself of everything—the burdens and frustrations and responsibilities, sending them all crashing down. He says I carry things around—the burdens of caring for others and through compassion feeling what they feel and crying it around—and sometimes I just need to let it all go, to momentarily let go of the weight, the burden, the responsibility. Let it all go.

We get curious and I find my Angry Part.

He's a little boy of about six and his small fists are raised in the air, shaking in frustration. Next to him, is an older female Maternal Part attempting to constrain him, telling him that anger is dangerous, that expressing it is unseemly and unacceptable.

The Maternal Part's constraint leads to more frustration

from the Little Boy Part. He wants to express himself when he wants to and to please the Constraining Maternal Part.

Bob has me take my Little Boy Part somewhere to let him be himself.

I take him to a boxing gym.

Unlike most of the boxing gyms I've seen, this one is new and pristine, all white and brightly lit.

The Little Boy Part goes over and begins punching the heavy bag with his little fists.

In a short period of time, he's hit the bag all he wants to, expressed himself, released his anger, and is now happily playing in the in the gym.

Bob observes that a boxing gym is the perfect place because anger is often held in and associated with the fists, and the fact that it's white means it's pure. The part is pure. The situation is pure. There's no trauma associated with the part.

I invite the Maternal Constraining Part to observe, and she sees how happy and free the Little Boy Part is and how good it is for him to express himself and his anger, how good it is for him not to be constrained or controlled.

She also witnesses the unblending that occurs with other parts and the Little Boy, and the unburdening that takes place when he lets go of the belief that it's not okay to express anger.

Toward the end of the session I share with Bob some of the family dynamics about not expressing anger that I had internalized.

Bob comments on what a good session this was and how he witnessed unblending and unburdening of parts. He also said how much it meant to him that I dedicated my most recent novel to him. He mention how he's always wanted to write a book and I tell him that I plan to write an IFS book one day and he seems very interested in the idea.

As we end the session, my Little Boy Part feels seen, safe, and free.

BOB'S NOTES

Anger is a fierce protector. It has different names and forms: frustration, rage, passive aggression, irritability, a visceral scream, the middle finger, a stomach ache, a clenched jaw.

When Anger hasn't been safe or permitted, we tend to turn it inwards on ourselves.

I have a history of ignoring my Anger. I will swallow it, discount it, deny it, run from it, push it away, and shame it.

I feel strongest when I allow it to reside inside my body and be felt and seen.

Allow your imagination to be curious about Anger. Notice what you find. The form doesn't matter.

It may be an image, a memory, a sound, a feeling, a voice, a color, or even a taste. It may live in a certain place inside your body or it may be very far away.

There's nothing you need to correct or change or fix about what you notice.

If another Part of you feels like Anger is getting too big or powerful, we can create a contained space for Anger. That could be a cottage whose door only opens from the outside, or a terrarium made of impenetrable glass that's bigger than a football field. Find what fits for you. What your Parts need.

When a Part needs containment for its own safety or the security of other Parts, we provide that. I like to make sure that there is a way to both see and communicate with the Part, so it knows it's not being abandoned. The Parts on the outside may need a way to control the volume. That can be accommodated.

Anger has its place. It must. If I doesn't it can consume us.

SESSION TWENTY-THREE

A certain man was preparing a great banquet and invited many guests.

When everything was ready, he sent his workers out to tell those who had been invited

"Come, for everything is now ready."

But they all began to make excuses, one after the other, for why they could not attend.

The workers reported this to the man throwing the party and it made him hurt and angry. "Go out quickly into the streets and alleys of the town and bring in the poor, the crippled, the blind and the lame so that my house will be full and we will have a grand celebration." — Jesus

"If you are lucky enough to have lived in Paris as a young man, then wherever you go for the rest of your life, it stays with you, for Paris is a moveable feast." — Ernest Hemingway

In my session with Bob today, we speak about my housing options.

I share with him what I'm thinking about and dealing with and trying to decide.

Building is going to take longer than I thought, so I'm considering selling my office building and RV camper and replacing them with a mobile home that I can live and work in until I build—after which, I'd have as a rental property.

We have a good bit of property and I have a few different options for where I could put a modular or mobile home.

Bob says it sounds like a lot of parts are actively speaking up about this.

I get curious and see there's a Manager Part trying to shepherd several different parts that all have things to say and all feel differently about my options.

Buying a mobile home will put a serious dent into the money I have in the bank—at least until I can sell the RV and office building.

Part of me wants to make sure that every choice I make enables me to continue to live how I have nearly my entire life—with a priority on family and loved ones, creativity, and spiritual practices.

I don't need a lot of money to do this, but I need enough—and I need to manage what I have well.

I'm experiencing some indecision—which is rare for me.

It's related to this season of change and transition and the unsettled and up-in-the-air nature of my existence during this time. And it's a good experience and practice for me. I've been so settled in so many ways for so long, this is a great shakeup.

There's a back-and-forth between my parts.

I tell Bob how I rarely feel indecisive, and I'm not used to it.

I can sell my office and RV and put a mobile home on the lot I'm on right now, which is across the street from where I am building. But this would involve selling and moving them prior to being able to move the mobile home in—and I'd be displaced for a while in between. Or, I could put the mobile home on another lot, which would take me farther away from where I'm building and put me close to another house we already have on that lot.

Bob asks what the indecisive part is fearful of or trying to protect.

I say it's fearful of and trying to protect me from making a mistake and getting locked into a situation that would take me away from my priorities and values and goals—way from the family time, writing, creating, and spiritual pursuits.

Another part of me says I needed to start spending less and living more frugally.

And a different part says that would mean doing less for others.

Bob asks if I can see myself living where I am right now in two years.

Part of me is saying to stay put, hold onto the money I have in the bank, while another is saying this is a temporary living situation and I can't keep living this way for much longer. Still another part of me knows that in the future I'll have more resources and income and a partner who will contribute to everything as well.

Bob asks me to take my activated parts to a place somewhere outside and sit with them.

Bob asks if there are other parts who need to say something, to check in with them and invite them to the table.

The moment he says this my indecision is gone.

Suddenly, I'm at a huge outdoor table with my parts.

It's a gathering, a feast, a celebration.

The banquet table is set up on one our lots across the street from our farm where I plan to build.

I have my answer. I'm feel free and unburdened, my noisy, conflicted, indecisive parts unblended.

Bob asks if part me is lonely.

A line from Jann Arden's "The Sound Of" drifts through my mind. "I am not lonely, swear to God I'm just alone."

I tell him I'm not lonely, but I do miss having a place to host gatherings, parties, music get-togethers, holiday celebrations with family and friends.

But I also need and enjoy my time alone.

I return to the gathering of my parts at the outside banquet table and enjoy the experience immensely.

INSIGHTS

Home for me has always been where my family is—this is most especially true of my children and grandchildren.

It has also meant having a place of my own, filled with my books and things, close to my extended family and loved ones in a particular geographic location.

I have a strong sense of place—particularly as a novelist whose work is centered in one region—but an even stronger sense of the people who inhabit that place.

This is what home is and has always been to me—and apart from 4 years in college, I have lived in the same area, surrounded by my family, my entire life.

This hasn't changed for me. But something inside me has.

Over the past decade or more I've been undergoing a shift, a recalibration, a transformation in orientation.

I am far more inward than outward oriented and directed.

And my sense and definition of home is among the many aspects of my existence this has been transformed—a process aided and enhanced by my children growing up and moving out and then eventually the sell of the house they grew up in.

My family and loved ones and to a lesser extent my

geographic location are still home to me. But now I have a deeper and more profound sense and experience of the home that is within me.

Wherever I am, I am home.

I am my home.

Home is within first, then without.

Turns out the old cliche that home is where the heart is is far more true and profound if taken literally. My heart is my home. From my heart (or Self) all other aspects of home flow.

The feast with my parts demonstrates this—as does seeing myself as Rumi's Guest House or being like a turtle or being a mansion that my Little Boy Part runs around and plays in.

I am my home as you are yours.

BOB'S NOTES

As I read Michael's reflections, a number of songs, sayings and metaphors about "home" and what "home" means came to mind. There are four places that I consider home. One is Big Bear, the town where I grew up. Another is San Diego, where I lived for 20 years. The third is Panama City where I currently live and am raising my own family. The final one is a place I only lived in for 10 months.

The summer between my junior and senior years in high school I had the opportunity to go to Japan for 3 weeks with a small group of students. While there I met exchange students from around the world and I realized that I also wanted to have that experience.

After I graduated from high school, I went to live in Brazil. I didn't get to choose the country I went to, but it ended up becoming a new home for me. In those 10 months I was opened up to living in (and FEELING in) a new family, language, and culture. I began to RELATE differently to myself, others and the world in general. I felt liberated.

When I came back to the U.S. to start college in San Diego, I wanted to make sure I didn't lose the "Brazilian Bob" that I had found. It has been a journey to keep rediscovering him. He is a feeling that goes beyond words.

In IFS, the "Self" is home. It never leaves us. It is always present but often gets obscured. "Brazilian Bob" is filled with Self energy, full of clarity and confidence. He is encapsulated by the Brazilian saying "tu que sabe" (you are that one that knows best).

What are your "homes." What do they feel like and what beliefs live there? Might there be homes you have yet to discover inside of you...

SESSION TWENTY-FOUR

He feels things deeply.

Passion. Compassion. Elation. Empathy.

As it says in a poem his mom once wrote about him for the celebration of a special occasion in his early twenties "what he likes, he loves."

The excitement he experiences is so intense it often finds expression in physical release—in dancing and jumping around and shouting for joy.

He is often moved to tears—in happiness and gratitude, far more frequently but no less intensely than in grief and pain.

His raw emotion often filters into and fires the kiln of his artistic expression.

And though he's a student, a reader and researcher, his spiritual experiences are mostly direct, experiential, mystical, and he feels he way through life, following his intuition.

But lately something's changed. He's not feeling the top and bottom ends as much.

It's as if the emotional equivalent of a vocal compressor has been turned on and it's limiting the highs above a certain level.

Perhaps it's affecting the lows as well, but it's on the highs that he notices it most.

He used to live mostly in the light, only visiting the Dark occasionally, and mostly through the portal of his imagination.

But now he's a dark figure in a dark alleyway in a downtown metropolis, and though the living, breathing city is pulsating around him, he's cleaving to the shadows of the empty alley next to the closed shops.

Away from the light and life of the city.

I share with Bob how lately I've been experiencing less elation, less intense joy than I usually do.

It could be how unsettled things are, could be the temporary nature of my living situation, all the changes and transitions taking place. Or it could be something physical or chemical. Whatever it is, I'm accustomed to feeling everything—especially joy and excitement and elation—more deeply than I have been lately.

Part of me is weary of my small and temporary living conditions and having my office/library in a separate space after having everything in one place (a place with plenty of space) for the past 25 years.

A different part of me is grateful for the experiences and opportunities I'm having and wants to learn all the lessons and soak up all the practices I can during this time, which will be over soon.

Part of me is trusting that I'm right where I need to be, embracing the unfolding, while another part of me is resisting and wanting things to be other than what they are.

And I have little doubt all of this is having an impact on my levels and experience of elation and joy.

But I also know this is to the weight of my nearly life long high expectations.

I share with Bob how I've been working on a new mystery thriller series over the past three years or so with a certain outcome in mind. I have been patiently developing the series in a certain way, producing a certain number of books over a particular period of time, in order to launch the series in a way that will give it the best chance of succeeding.

But even with all I've done, all my hard work and patience, there are several steps that have to happen that are completely out of my control. It's entirely possible for me to do all I can and this still now work.

But it did. It worked exactly according to plan, and all the aspects of it that were out of my control lined up perfectly too.

It's hard to imagine it working any better than it did. It was as if everything I conceived of and hoped for 3 years ago happened just like I wanted it to.

And though I'm truly grateful and happy about it, I'm not as thrilled or elated as I usually am, as I have been in the past.

And I wonder if how much of my muted response is related to the changes and transitions I'm experiencing and my current living situation and how much of it is related to other factors, such as aging or the fact that something similar to this has happened before.

Bob says he senses a lot of blending.

He goes onto explain that when parts blend there can be less clarity, which can lead to less joy and some of the other feelings and experiences I'm describing.

We get curious.

A Dissatisfied Mid-Twenties Part in a stylish suit comes forward.

He's living in Buckhead in Atlanta.

The bright lights of the big city turn the dark night to day beneath a thumbnail moon, but he's standing in the shadow two tall buildings cast into an alleyway.

His energy matches that of the city as it hums impatiently through him.

He's assertive and occasionally aggressive, and gets things done by the sheer force of his strong will.

Bob asks if he's an alternate version of me.

I find the question interesting—especially when I hear the part's response to how he sees me. According to him, I'm around his age and also in a suit—but instead of a shirt and tie I'm in a clerical collar and taking a much more gentle, relaxed approach to life as a young father and minister.

Bob asks me to let the part see me as I am now and spend some time together.

I go to him in the dark alley.

After seeing who I am now he trusts me enough to leave the dark alley. We walk to a nearby park, a green oasis tucked into the urban jungle. Unlike the alleyway, it's well lit, and it's calming and restorative to be surrounded by nature.

The Dissatisfied Mid-Twenties Part says he doesn't want to sit down and he doesn't want an older man telling him what to do or how to live. He tells me if I regret something that's on me. I had my opportunities. Don't put any of that on him.

Eventually, he takes a seat beside me and sees me more clearly.

Rather than regret he sees happiness and settledness. Rather than anxious impatience he sees calm. And he realizes I'm not here to tell him how to live or what to do.

He's intrigued by my calm, relaxed approach to life, especially when he sees just how much I still accomplish.

The part is beginning to experience a shift in perspective, a change, a transformation.

But he's still suspicious.

He still has questions, but he's more open than he was before.

He says he's willing to try new things, to attempt a different approach.

Bob asks if there's a place he'd like to live and what job he'd like to do.

He says he wants to do the same job, that he's good at managing and getting things accomplished, but that he'd like to do it without oppressive deadlines and pressure and stress.

I remove the ticking clock from his work.

He then says he'd like to stay in the city, but be in a smaller neighborhood, similar to a small town, that has everything he needs, so he won't have to continue rushing all over the metro area.

I put him in a nice area with a thriving arts district.

Bob brings up Eric Erickson's eight stages of life—1) infancy Basic trust versus mistrust, 2) Toddler – autonomy versus shame and doubt, 3) Preschool-age – initiative versus guilt, 4) School-age – industry versus inferiority, 5) Adolescence – identity versus identity confusion, 6) Young adulthood – intimacy versus isolation, 7) Middle age – generativity versus stagnation, 8) Older adulthood – integrity versus despair—and questions if this has anything to do with the stage of life that I'm in.

INSIGHTS

As I reflect on this period of time when I wasn't experiencing elation and joy to the same level I almost always had, I see that it was a little related to age and stage of life, but mostly the situation I was in at that time.

It had far more to do with being uprooted after 25 years in the same home and living in tiny and temporary quarters and all the changes and transitions I had gone through in the past five years and I was still going through.

In many ways I felt like I was living in limbo.

Bob asked if any of this was related to a previous relationship and partner.

I told him I sure some of it was—after all, I wouldn't have been in that exact situation if I hadn't ended that relationship—but it was negligible and had far more to do with the change and transition involved than the ending of the relationship itself, which brought a great sense of relief and joy. I had taken on far too much responsibility for the relationship and the other person and was trying to make it work in spite of the other person suffering from issues and conditions that led to periodic days-long episodes of outrageous and toxic behaviors and cruelty. These were followed by seemingly sincere apologies and assurances that she'd get help and make changes, and sandwiched in between periods of support, acts of kindness, expressions of deep love, and effusive praise. And I was grateful to no longer be on that Jekyll and Hyde rollercoaster.

I told Bob that something about the place where the part was standing reminded me of this previous partner saying she was not going to live in my shadow, not be the Robin to my Batman.

Another aspect of the experience with the Dissatisfied Mid-Twenties Part in the shadows of the city was the pace and pulse and energy of the city—the dissatisfaction and the relentless pressure to produce, to always be striving to do and be more. It reminded me of certain pushy people earlier in my life—always pushing, always pressing, always wanting something, and how my sensitivity to others and my desire for them to experience serenity and joy interacted with this Dissatisfied Mid-Twenties Part and the People-Pleasing Part of me.

BOB'S NOTES

A fundamental question that brings many people to therapy is, "Where do I belong?" As Erik Erikson show us, this search for belonging evolves as we go through different stages of life.

Because our Parts often exist in different ages/stages, the nature of the "belonging" that they are seeking may vary. As we begin to connect with Parts, we can ask them questions like:

"Where do you belong?"

"Where would you like to belong?"

"Have you ever lost a sense of belonging or felt abandoned?"

As I explore this with my clients, in the back of my mind I remember that the belonging the Parts are searching for is already there. It is Self energy. As they begin unblending that Self energy often becomes apparent.

Yesterday I met with a woman in her mid 40s. We have been working with Parts grieving the death of her father when she was 8. This 8 year old girl carried a belief that it was her fault that her dad had died. She had prayed to God to save him. Because the 8 year old believed "God answers prayers," she deduced it must be her fault that he didn't answer her prayer. A

Part of the girl was angry at God, but one of the girl's beliefs was, "You can't be angry at God."

Anger was banished. She described it as a "darkness" that was "supposed to stay hidden and not be seen." It had no place to belong.

So we sat in the darkness with Anger. We didn't demand anything from it. As it began to trust and feel my client's Self energy emerging, it told us its purpose. It wanted to be a "bodyguard" and expose the truth that it is "not evil."

It discovered where it belonged.

SESSION TWENTY-FIVE

She's three years younger than him, his little sister, his best friend.

Inseparable, they do everything together. But she doesn't just tag along. He invites her, brings her, treats her like a peer.

If the kids his age don't want her around, then he doesn't play with them, choosing instead his little sister.

He loves her and she adores him. He is her hero, her idol.

Other adults tell their mom they can't believe they're siblings. They don't fight like siblings. He doesn't not want her around like most older brothers.

He sees her not only as his little sister and best friend, but his responsibility. It's his duty and honor to look out for her, protect her, keep her as safe as their parents do when they're around.

Today I share with Bob how I'm continuing to examine myself for patterns of thinking and behavior that don't serve me well—specifically in the realm of relationships.

I try to do this with every area of my life—take a close, honest look at what's really going on within and without and the results, the fruit that the tree of my life is producing.

And though I've done this for nearly as long as I can remember, it's only recently that I'm doing it within the framework of IFS and the milieu of parts work.

A close examination of my adult relationships reveals some patterns that I'm very pleased with and wouldn't change for anything and a few others that I've been in the process of changing for several years. And though I feel like I've been mostly successful at addressing these issues and making these changes I want to ensure that's the case by doing the underlying parts work related to them.

I not only want to have an intellectual and emotional understanding, but an experiential wisdom that includes head and heart, mind and body.

For context, over the past several years, here are some of what I've been exploring and addressing: my desire to heal, help, rescue and take responsibility for others, my propensity to project onto others characteristics and traits that aren't there and to ignore the red flags that are, my approaching my relationships in a similar manner to my compassion-based calling/vocation as a minister, counselor, and teacher, my impatience, romanticism, idealism, and cultural and religious indoctrination, my tendency to get too serious and assume too much responsibility too quickly, my misguided sense of duty, honor, and responsibility, my desire to avoid conflict as much as possible, my sincere and misguided belief that unconditional love alone is enough to ultimately create an environment for healing and change for others—and that it's my responsibility to practice that, to create that environment, and my embarrassment, guilt, and shame at a relationship not working.

All of these dynamics haven't been present in all my relationships and most or all are no longer present much at all—at least to the degree they were in the past, but my Figure-Outer Part wants to, well, figure it out why they ever were.

I start by telling Bob that I'm most curious why I stayed

with a previous partner as long as I did, why I was willing to ride the Jekyll and Hyde rollercoaster at the center of her particular internal theme park.

Intellectually, I know why. I made a commitment. I felt a responsibility. I believed her apologies and her proclamations that she would get help and get better, her Dr. Jekyll phases were largely good and she was mostly sweet, supportive, fun and often adoring and effusive with the lavishing of her love. I believed in my ability to make it work and that with enough time and unconditional love she would heal. I was taking responsibility for the relationship and I thought her seemingly sincere apologies that followed every episode and meltdown meant she was taking reasonability for herself, her healing and growth.

Eventually, of course, I saw there was very little happening besides apologies and acts of contrition. There was some reading and some journaling and lots and lots of long conversations, but her promises of seeing a therapist and the possibility of taking medication were ultimately empty.

Bob says he's hearing responsible and overly responsible parts.

He asks me to get curious and to investigate where I'm feeling this in my body.

When I get curious and go within, I immediately sense a beautiful pink, sunset glow of spiritual energy flowing from my heart. Rooted in love and compassion and empathy, it's a desire to heal and care of others. It's pure and powerful.

Next to it, is an Overly Responsible Manager Part that says his job is to make sure that my heart stays open and to remind me and other parts of me to take care of others, to give and do for others, to share that enormous love energy with them.

This part reminds me of the scripture "to whom much is given, much is required," and that I've been given so much love that it's my duty and responsibility to share it with others—

especially those who weren't given what I was, that it's my responsibility to share this gift, to try to make up for what others lack, to help them and heal them.

Back in my head and inside memories, I share with Bob how as long as I can remember I've felt compassion for and in someways responsible for the marginalized and disenfranchised. Growing up as a straight, white guy in the deep South, my heart went out to and I befriended those I perceived as treated unjustly as other—African-American, gay, different. And I think this is a big part of why I was so drawn to the historical Jesus, the bastard peasant and subversive sage who was intimate with sinners, misfits, and outcasts and Dr. King, the poetic prophet and oracle martyr, who was slain the year I was born.

Growing up, the Overly Responsible Manager Part of me felt white and majority and male and middle-class guilt.

The babysitters and caregivers who assisted my parents in caring for me during my formative years and beyond were older African-American women who I loved and adored and identified with.

Bob says he hears empathy.

I share with him how I also grew up with a deep sense of responsibility for my little sister, and how I felt like it was my job to protect and care for her. I recall my parents and grandparents and others saying what a great big brother I was—and one grandparent saying I did too much, took too much responsibility for her. And I think about the positive feedback and affirmation I received for being a responsible big brother caregiver.

As I ponder this, I think about birth order and the fact that until my current relationship, every single woman I've been involved with was the baby of the family or an only child. I find this instructive and significant, and believe that I'm now in a relationship with another firstborn speaks to my growth and transformation.

I tell Bob how this Overly Responsible Manager Part can be judgmental of those he deems as irresponsible, particularly parents.

As we reach the end of the session and have to stop for now, I know there is much more parts work to be done in this area and I look forward to returning to it.

INSIGHTS

When I was fresh out of my small-town high school, my parents took me to Atalanta to tour the ministerial college I wanted to attend. The tour included the recruiter and the registrar showing us what they loosely called the dorm—a large unit in an older apartment complex known for poverty, drugs, gangs, and violence.

When the danger in living in such a place came up and the recruiter and registrar remarked that the ministerial students residing here would need to be responsible and careful, my dad expressed to them that I, at 18, was already one of the most responsible people he knew and that he trusted me with his life.

I've been a responsible, perhaps even overly-responsible person for as long as I can remember.

And though for much of my life I didn't give it much thought, if I had, I think I would've thought that being responsible was about being strong and chivalrous, caring and empathic, and having integrity.

Parts of me sincerely believed that in the same way that I had an abundance of love to spare and it was my calling/duty/obligation to share it, I was responsible for being responsible also.

I see it quite differently now.

Now, in many ways, I see my relationship to responsibility as one of misunderstanding and transgression, instead of compassion and heroism.

I now see that in some instances I have actually been guilty of taking responsibility for and from others and not merely accepting it for myself.

And only in recent years have I come to see just how wrong I've been to do so.

It's fascinating that I didn't always do this—didn't always take far more than my fair share of the responsibility, didn't always do it the same way even when I did. In some relationships I've taken little to no responsibility for the other person and only more or less my part of the responsibility for the relationships itself.

This means that it changed as situations and dynamics and needs and personalities changed. The way I see it now, in some circumstances my Overly Responsible Parts were more activated, burdened, and blended than others.

I once asked one of my closest friends what would happen if I stopped reaching out and organizing gatherings—because I was about the only one in our group doing it. He said no one else did it because they knew I would, and I ever stopped doing it one of them would pick up the slack.

When this was put to the test it mostly proved that what he was saying was untrue, but I think it says something about the way some of the responsibility dynamics of some relationships work.

Regardless, my focus is on the how's and why's and when's and who's involved in my parts causing me to become overly responsible—particularly for other people.

As the term implies, *taking* responsibility involves the act of capturing, gaining possession, and dispossessing someone of something.

And that *something* I was dispossessing them of was their own responsibility and culpability.

It was so easy for me, as the responsible firstborn son, to go from taking care of and feeling responsible for my little sister, to extending that to certain others—especially as a young minister, counselor, chaplain, and even later as a teacher, friend, and significant other, particularly given certain situations and needful dynamics.

Without nearly enough awareness, my sense of responsibility and genuine desire to help and heal became in certain situations a kind of chivalric response to a damsel in distress.

Instead of merely and fully and only accepting responsibility for myself I was taking it for and from others. My practice on all fronts, including IFS parts work has been to stop taking it for others and only accept it for me.

BOB'S NOTES

Today Michael describes a Part (or Parts) whose purpose is to be responsible for others. That's how the Part(s) experiences a sense of belonging.

We wouldn't want to ask this Part to stop doing what it believes it's meant to do. If we did, it would go into hiding and "darkness" as Anger did for the client I spoke about last session.

If you do a Google search using "Bob Newhart Stop It" you will find a 6 minute clip that shows his psychiatrist character using the completely opposite approach. It's funny. It's also kind of tragic.

Most of us have Parts that have experienced this message.

Stop. Go Away. Usually that message is coming from another Part . . . or even Legacy.Often their purpose is to stop us from making mistakes . . . at all costs.

Never again.

In the last session my client's "Angry" Part experienced a sense of belonging by being witnessed as the "Bodyguard" it was meant to be. Interestingly, the Bodyguard had a male identity. As we continued working with this Part, I asked if there was anything it would like to let go of, and if so how would they be released; to the air, water, earth, fire, light or anywhere else.

My client's Bodyguard began describing these rocks he was carrying and said he'd like to release them into the water. The rocks were the old beliefs that burdened him. That she was evil, bad, and needed to stay hidden.

She let them go. And was freed.

SESSION TWENTY-SIX

A grand old mansion.
High ceilings. Huge rooms. Vast chambers. Endless corridors. Expansive staircases.
Servants. Guests.
A busy mom and dad.
Average day. Adults going about their business.
All adults, save one child.
A little boy playing alone.
He sees mostly their feet and lower legs, the occasional quick shadow of them passing by.
Do they see him at all?
Running down long, empty corridors. Hiding under enormous banquet tables. Pretending. Fantasizing. Daydreaming.
His home is a castle, a fort, a forest, a jungle, a city, a universe, and, expanded by his limitless imagination, his world entire.
In my session with Bob today I share how before the backdrop of delving into and practicing amor fati, I have been looking at the sense of expectation I've had as a young person.

Amor fati means "love of fate," the welcoming and embracing of all of life's various experiences as good—or at least as inevitable, immutable.

I enter today's session curious about why I've always had such high expectations.

There have been times over the course of my life, particularly when I was younger, that my great expectations were a source of impatient frustration.

I addressed this in a variety of ways, beginning with accepting of what is, then concentrating and embracing, and appreciating the journey, the process, and letting go of all else, and then relinquishing my attachment to outcomes. Essentially, practicing Dr. Reinhold Niebuhr's Serenity prayer.

O God grant me...

the Serenity to accept the things I cannot change;

the Courage to change the things I can,

and the Wisdom to know the difference, Amen.

When I practice this I find the serenity that comes from letting go—letting go of obsessing, of the illusion of control, of the belief that I can make things happen by will and work.

I get curious and go within.

A Seven-Year-Old Boy Part is present

He is idealistic, romantic, imaginative—a storyteller with an audience of one. Himself.

He's a thinker and a daydreamer.

I have a memory of me at that age—of my parents being on a date and my grandmother keeping me and my little sister.

As my sister and grandmother watched TV, I pretended that I was an adult, a single detective, living in an apartment building in a city. My bedroom was my apartment, which I pretended to lock and unlock with a ring of keys I had from my Dad's hardware store. And the living room where my sister and grandmother were watching TV was the common room inside the apartment building. I would go in and out of that room, pretending they were my neighbors. My go-kart was my car, my treehouse was a drive-in movie theater, and the imagined woman in the seat next to me was my wife.

Bob asks how this part sees me now.

I ask him, but he doesn't respond.

He's busy playing, concentrating on what he's pretending, in his own little world, uninterested in the world outside of his world, which includes me.

Bob asks to let him lead me to a place where he's like to go and where we can hang out. He leads me to his treehouse, the huge, tall treehouse his dad built him with light poles around a large oak tree.

He sees me as an older teenager.

He's very creative, idealistic, and romantic, but all in an internal, self-directed way.

He doesn't really care much about what's going on outside of his own mind, his own world, the world he creates. Yet he doesn't feel disconnected because everything he does is within the context of a loving, supportive family and a safe home, where he is both free and secure.

Bob says he's a story maker.

Not a storyteller, a story maker.

He seems to need nothing or want anything, just to be and create.

I picture myself as a mansion where all my parts live and also as the Little Boy Part allowed to run around and play and do his own thing—in the context of being cared for and protected by the other parts.

Some parts mostly ignore him. Others say he needs to be more practical, needs to grow up, and not spend so much time playing and daydreaming.

I ask Bob if it's possible the Little Boy Part is an exile. I don't think he is, and I believe he has a lot of Self-like energy, but I'm curious.

I don't ask the Little Boy Part to change in any way, or do anything differently, and I hope to visit him again as I explore my mind mansion more in the future.

INSIGHTS

The mansion in this session made me think of a memory palace—an imaginary location in our minds where we can store mnemonic images.

This technique is believed by many to have been created by Simonides of Ceos some 2,500 years ago, though the method of loci (Latin for location) can actually be traced back to hunter gatherer times and found in many cultures.

Often, memory palaces involve making a journey through a place we know well and always visiting the locations same order.

The mansion in my mind today also and inevitably made me think of Rumi's guest house again.

This being human is a guest house.
    Every morning a new arrival.

A joy, a depression, a meanness,
    some momentary awareness comes
    As an unexpected visitor.
    Welcome and entertain them all!

Even if they're a crowd of sorrows,
    who violently sweep your house
    empty of its furniture,
    still treat each guest honorably.
    He may be clearing you out
    for some new delight.

The dark thought, the shame, the malice,
    meet them at the door laughing,
    and invite them in.

Be grateful for whoever comes,
    because each has been sent
    as a guide from beyond.

I am my mansion, my memory palace. My parts are its guests and inhabitants.

BOB'S NOTES

"Never again!"

Our Parts that are protective managers want to ensure that we don't have to go back "there." And they have good reason to keep us from memories and experiences of trauma. The challenge is that they also keep us from remembering the other parts as well.

The word "remember" speaks to putting the "members" back together. Finding the puzzle pieces that have been dropped on the floor and swept under the couch.

Each puzzle piece is a part of the whole. An important piece of the map.

As we discover these Parts, we often find that they also have Parts within them that are trying to help them negotiate their memories and the energy they feel from the other Parts around them.

As Michael found, each Part might live in its own mansion. Would it like to give a tour? Can we offer the open hand of curiosity and calm to encourage it to lead the way? Joining it, even when it runs into a dark corridor or locked room. Helping it find remember it is not alone. Self energy can help it find the keys and turn on lights.

SESSION TWENTY-SEVEN

The sweaty HVAC tech climbs down out of his van, an apologetic expression beneath his sweat-stained, company-branded ball cap.

"Sorry I'm late," the HVAC tech says.

He's running late today, it's true—his arrival is over two hours after the appointment time. But he's not jus running a couple of hours late for today's appointment. He's actually severals days late, making and breaking several appointments over the past week or so.

And it's not just that he's running late to install the new HVAC system in the new house, it's that it leads to delays with other subcontractors and ultimately to being able to move in.

"No problem, the new homeowner says. "All good."

He's been waiting patiently, occupying his mind and his time with thinking, reading, mediating, working, being present —instead of waiting impatiently, focused on the waiting itself.

Earlier in life he was known for his impatience. He rushed from thing to thing and heated waiting for anything. But over the years, his spiritual practices, psychological work, and life itself (including the aging process), has led him to slow down and let go. It's not always the case, of course, there are times when he reverts back to frustrated impatience, but it's increasingly rare. And these days more often that not if someone makes a comment at all it's about his patience and serenity.

"I appreciate you being so patient. It's really rare. Most all the other customers are constantly calling, rushing us, complaining, never happy. But you're so calm and chill and patient. Can't tell you how much better that makes my job."

He has learned, is continuing to learn, that getting upset, angry, or frustrated doesn't make anything happen any faster. It merely serves to steals his serenity.

I share with Bob how I have been complemented on my patience several times lately.

Impatience has been such a weakness of mine for so long—and such an emphasis in my self-development and work—that it's nice to not only see the change but have it confirmed.

Being in between homes and living in an RV camper for six months has taught me, among many other things, patience. So has all my work on my new home.

I can honestly say that I'm being patient during this process, letting go, and embracing the unfolding. And, in fact, the air conditioner man commented on how patient and calm I have been just this week.

We talk about this for a while, especially, at first, my sense of calm.

I was with a group of friends having dinner recently and somehow the topic of fears and comfort levels came up, and one of the women there said I always seem at peace and at ease, comfortable and confident in every situation she's seen me in. She went on to say that she couldn't imagine me ever feeling anything other than calm and confident because she's never seen me be anything but—including while doing things that frighten other people, such as public speaking, especially officiating funerals and weddings, sharing personal things and being vulnerable, counseling and helping the dying, the bereaved, the incarcerated.

I was moved and touched by her observations and kind comments—and surprised that she had observed me at all, let alone given what she had perceived any thought.

I tell Bob that as much as what she said resonates with me, and as much as I'm grateful for my growth in this area, it's the times I feel self-conscious, even if it doesn't show, that I'd like to explore.

When I get curious, I encounter an Adolescent Part who is shy, quiet, and easily embarrassed. He doesn't like attention or the spotlight, doesn't like criticism and conflict.

I begin to see how this part is related to being sensitive and an introvert and caring too much about the perceptions of others. It also has legacy elements—I definitely see it in other family members.

An Older Part immediately begins to give him advice for how not to be bothered by any of that.

I share with Bob how this sense of embarrassment can happen with effusive praise as much as criticism.

This entire dynamic is also related to feeling things deeply, passionately, profoundly, and taking an essentially serious approach to life. Not surprisingly it's related to my over sense of responsibility as well.

I play and laugh a lot with family and close friends. My novels are infused with humor. But I tend toward the serious end of the spectrum between tragedy and comedy.

We talk about the foolishness of faith, of living intuitively, of making a living making up stories, and how all the wisdom traditions have at their center a fool. I embrace this and do much that is foolish but can also be embarrassed by it.

Bob asks me to take the parts somewhere for them to relax and hang out and talk.

The Adolescent Part immediately asks if we can go to the state park.

Interestingly, when I was a teenager the state park was sacred to me. It was where I went to think and pray and meditate and to process everything.

It was secluded and serene and nearly always empty.

It was my sanctuary, my sacred space—until the county took it over from the state and cut down many of the trees and a Cat 5 hurricane took out the rest.

We go to the state park that still exists inside of me, and sit at the top of the hill that slopes down to a pond. We're beneath a couple of pines, surrounded by the pine needles and pine cones that have fallen from the trees to join us on the ground.

The Adolescent Part sees who I was now, experiences the calmness and settledness and confidence of Self. Healing and reassuring of the Adolescent Part occurs.

I tell Bob that if I experience any embarrassment or self-conscious these days it's most often related to doing something new.

He says that newness brings with it vulnerability and reminds me that most everything is new to my Adolescent Part.

BOB'S NOTES

We have to respect a Part's pace. Some are ready to turn on all the lights in the mansion, while others aren't sure if they even want to knock on the front door.

One of my dad's sayings is, "Hurry up and go slow." In a way it acknowledges my Parts that want to get things done and make progress while also reminding them that sometimes they best way to make that progress is to go slow.

Another therapist I know said it this way. "So much to do. So little time. Better go slow."

It's about attunement, respect, and trust. As a therapist, I want to empower my clients . . . meaning I give them the power to set the pace as I attune to them and their Parts. In my own inside world, I respect my Parts by doing the same thing.

SESSION TWENTY-EIGHT

"I shall be miserable if I have not an excellent library." —Jane Austen

"A room without books is like a body without a soul." Cicero

He's had his own library since he was a teenager, small at first, a single shelf, then a full bookcase, then another, then another.

A few shelves in his dorm room in college turned into a dedicated room in his first house. The formal living room of his second home became the largest library he ever had, and for a quarter of a century, he lived and worked mostly in that space. A hundred books turned into a thousand, a thousand into ten thousand, ten thousand into tens of thousands.

Always in a sacred, dedicated space, a library in his home.

Until now.

Now, in his new home, there's not a single room large enough for his library.

He has a library in it, a dedicated, sacred space, but it can only hold about half of his books.

In his new place, books spill out of his library, tumble down the hallway, and take up residence in every room.

He no longer has a house with a library in it, but a home that is a library.

Today, I share with Bob how I'm continuing to explore and examine what I'm doing with my life, with my time.

It's something I've done as long as I can remember, something I do on a continual basis.

As part of this most recent inquiry into what I'm doing with the gift of my life, I'm questioning, among other things, my independence.

Very much an introverted individual traveling my own path, at times alone, at times with a few others, mostly family and close friends, I wonder, not for the first time, if I'm too independent.

I've never been much of a joiner, never found a group or organization that quite fit.

I go at it alone. Not completely alone, of course. I have a very close family and a few very close friends, and a cloud of witnesses, a spiritual community that journey with me largely through the books they have written and the recordings of their talks and teachings. And I have a network of friends and colleagues, many of whom are hundreds and thousands of miles away.

But is this enough? Should I be part of a more defined and local community or organization?

I reflect on how in earlier life, for a brief time, I attempted to be part of certain groups and organizations, and how my introvertedness, impatience, idealism, and my particular creative and idiosyncratic path made it a challenge.

When I get curious a Twenty-something Young Man Part asks why I have both an undergraduate and graduate degree in theology that I do so little with.

I was once a minister, a prison chaplain, an adjunct religion professor, but now I'm mostly a novelist and songwriter with only a limited time left for giving inspirational talks and spiritual teachings.

Bob asks how I feel toward the part that is asking this question.

I say that I love and appreciate him, his questioning, his energy, his exuberance—and the fact that he lives with a sense of calling, purpose, and mission. And I appreciate that his questioning is loving and gentle, not critical or judgmental.

Bob asks me to have the part come sit beside me.

As he does, I see that he's my Figure-Outter/Seeker Part. He has a pen and a pad and is leaning forward, inquiring, poised to take notes, to find answers and figure out things.

I ask him to relax, to put down his pen and paper and sit back.

Bob asks me to do a body scan and to breathe slowly and relax.

As I do, I realize that congestion in my chest and head are preventing me from breathing deeply, impeding the peaceful place I'm trying to relax and breathe into. I feel stuffed up and stuck.

I tell all my parts to just be—not to do anything, no work, no jobs, just relax and breathe with me.

Calmness comes.

After a while Bob asks about the possibility of me teaching at the college again.

I tell him I've certainly considered it. And that in addition to giving more inspirational and spiritual talks, I've always wanted to have a retreat center, to conduct spiritual growth, enlightenment, artist, creative, and writing retreats.

I share with Bob how I believe the questioning and exploring I've been doing that led to the topic of this session is related to me moving my books my library into my new home this week.

Handling my books, touching each one, vividly reminded me that about half are in the areas of theology, religion, spirituality, psychology, and self-help.

I tell him that for the first time ever my library is not limited to a single room in my home, but is now unbound and spills out into all the rooms and how different that is for me.

As much as I love having a dedicated library space, I'm also loving the way that my entire home is also a library.

He says the word "exposure" comes to mind.

I say I like the exposure I'm getting to my books no matter which room I'm in, and the way my family and friends are also exposed to them without ever having to go into my library.

My books spill out of my library into every room in my home, into every aspect of my life, as what I do, writing, teaching, speaking, counseling, making music, spills out of me into every aspect of my life.

INSIGHTS

Recently, I had the great privilege and honor to officiate my son and his fiancé's wedding. I used story as the theme and created a book of their story that I gave to them once the ceremony concluded.

Here are a few snippets from what I wrote for their sacred ceremony.

Every life is a story. In a certain sense we are all books in the library of life, protagonists of our own stories, heroes on journeys that are simultaneously similar to those of others and uniquely our own.

Sometimes our stories intersect and we play pivotal roles in each other stories. We are here today because this has happed for two people we love more than words, and who's stories we cherish as much as our own.

"Listen," Mia Couto said, "and you will realize that we are made not from cells or from atoms, but from stories."

To differing degrees each of us here, have been part of Micah's and Ashley's stories and they a part of ours. We've given birth to them, raised them, watched them grow up, overcome adversity, experience the full pain and joy of life, and become who they are standing here today.

Once upon a time is every time. It's this time and all the times that led to this time, to this moment.

The journey Micah and Ashley have been on—every path, every experience, every choice, every response and reaction and decision led them to each other.

Rumi said "The minute I heard my first love story, I started looking for you, not knowing how blind that was. Lovers don't finally meet somewhere. They're in each other all along."

They met when they were ready to meet, when all their preparation to meet was complete, in July of 2021.

This book I hold is a book of life—the story of Micah and Ashley and the life they share. It is filled with photos and notes, texts and treasures, and the words and vows of this ceremony. Prior to this ceremony, Ashley and Micah's parents and siblings have penned pages and added them to this book and now Micah and Ashley will add their pages to this book, which following the ceremony will become theirs for them to add pages to for years to come.

Micah and Ashley your individual stories have been joined, and now paper from the tree of life becomes pages in the book of life, your life together, your combined epic, romantic, thrilling, fulfilling love story is now one. One book. One life. One love.

BOB'S NOTES

I have Parts that like to clean the house. Sometimes I even look forward to it or fantasize about what it might feel like if everything is "in its place."

—Put together a box or two of things we no longer need and donate it to the good will.
—Reorganize the furniture.
—Empty the trash.
—Sweep the floor.
—Put the 50 things that have gathered on the counters and spilled over onto any open space.

It has something to do with having a sense of agency regarding my surroundings. Mostly it's about creating safety in a physical form.

I imagine Michael "nesting" with all of his books. Each book a twig or leaf that gives form to something meaningful.

But is it the form itself that matters? Or is it more the process of creating and shifting the form to fit what Parts need to feel safe.

What does your space look like . . . or, better yet, what does it FEEL like?

SESSION TWENTY-NINE

A dark, rainy night in South Florida.

A Spanish-style bungalow with a terracotta tile roof. Inside, light and cool and dry. Outside, unseen in the shadows, a sentry stands watch in the damp darkness.

He doesn't care that his clothes are soaked through. Or that he's hungry and thirsty. Or that misquotes are biting him. He only cares about his mission.

His mission, his purpose in life is to protect, to stand watch —to look out for and guard the little boy inside that bungalow. Something he mostly does from the shadows

When Bob and I get curious today, I see a Protector Part, sort of standing to the side, next to the Younger Part he's protecting.

It's a damp, rainy night and the Protector is in the shadows standing watching for a Little Boy Part he believes needs protecting.

The Little Boy Part is inside a Sought Florida bungalow on a stormy night and the Protector Part is outside in the elements.

The Little Boy is unaware that the Protector is there.

My Figure-Outter Part wonders why South Florida, why a bungalow. Is there meaning and significance behind it? If so, he doesn't know what it is.

I ask the Figure-Outter Part to step aside and not attempt to figure anything out right now.

The Protector Part is unfazed by the elements. He's strong and tough and on a mission. His job is to protect the vulnerable, young part, and he derives great satisfaction from it.

When I ask the Protector Part to come away with me, he says he will, seems agreeable, but remains standing watch.

He moves slightly, like he's coming with me, but doesn't move much, and ultimately stays where he is, doing what he has been doing.

He feels a high degree of responsibility in his job as protector.

Complicating everything else, my Figure-Outter Part won't quite stop doing his job either, continuing, somewhat in the background to try to figure out the setting and why the Protector is there, outside, in the elements, like an unseen operative and bodyguard. Lurking. Watching.

Bob asks why the Protector is doing his job in such a way that the younger part doesn't know he's being protected.

The Protector Part responds that it's his way of protecting the feelings of the Little Boy Part he's protecting.

He's very much a Dad-like Part, who can handle anything is not bothered by the elements or anything else, and doesn't want any credit or recognition for doing his job.

This part is the most stubborn part I've had, and the first part to refuse, in action at least, to stop what he's doing and join me somewhere else.

I decide to leave him in place, doing his job, and to be more aware of him and revisit him in the future.

Bob says there's a lot of Self-like energy in the part, which makes sense—I identify as a dad, a father, more than anything else—and it's no wonder he doesn't want to stop doing his job, even for a moment.

INSIGHTS

Like you, I am a lot of things.

I'm a novelist, a writer, a creative, an inspirational speaker, a singer-songwriter, a thinker, a lover, a reader, a giver, a healer, a teacher, a basketball player, a friend, a son, an uncle, and on and on, but mostly I'm a dad and a Grandude.

It's not surprisingly to me that my dad-like protector part won't leave his post. It's also not surprising that he's willing to stand out in the rain and elements keeping watch.

I am many things. But I am first and foremost a dad.

I'm not surprised that many of my most self-like parts have dad-like qualities. But I am surprised of the setting involved in this session. I live in North not South or Central Florida. And though I have visited those parts of my state many times, I've never been to a place quite like the one from this session.

Like many of the locations involved in my parts work, this one is something out of a dream.

I see parts work as akin to dream work. We tap into something deep inside us in the same way dreams do.

"All that we see or seem is but a dream within a dream."
— Edgar Allan Poe

BOB'S NOTES

What is the difference between stubborn and confident . . . or between arrogance and courage?

I find that confidence and courage are qualities of Self energy that tend to be more difficult to identify and discover.

So many of us carry self doubt, and we are quick to dismiss ourselves. Parts have received messages that when we stand up for ourselves and stand our ground we are being stubborn or difficulty or arrogant.

In this session Michael respected the voice of the Protector who refused to leave his station. As he did that he discovered it carried Self energy.

What Parts do you have that might be waiting to be respected or honored? What might they want to tell you? How do they respond when validated? Can you feel their confidence and courage?

SESSION THIRTY

"Your task is not to seek for love, but to seek and find all the barriers you have built against it." —Rumi

I share with Bob how I'm preparing an inspirational talk I'm giving on Sunday and would like to explore the subject with him.

The topic is "A Love that Liberates."

When we get curious two parts come forward—a Little Boy Part and an Older Protector Part.

Both parts are inside a membrane-like covering like a cocoon or a womb.

As I see more I see that it is a womb.

Bob has me show them who I am.

The warm glow of love and energy flows from Self to them.

And a shift occurred.

Rather than believing I'm the same age as they are, they see me as I am now, and this changes everything—their perceptions and beliefs and world views.

They emerge from their cocoon-womb, birthed out of their barrier, very, very slowly.

This birthing process has them following sunlight out of a save and into a field.

Turning toward the sun, moving closer, soaking up its powerful, warm rays. The Little Boy begins to run and play in the field. The Older Part joins in, though more slowly.

Safe. Secure. Happy. Free. Loved and loving.

Outside of their womb and in the light of Self they both say they have need of nothing, that everything they need is within them.

Neither part wants to leave the field. Neither wants a job for now. They just want to enjoy their freedom.

Bob says that reminds him of another Rumi quote, which I, too, am thinking of.

"Out beyond ideas of wrongdoing and rightdoing,
There is a field. I'll meet you there.
When the soul lies down in that grass,
The world is too full to talk about.
Ideas, language, even the phrase each other
Doesn't make any sense." —Rumi

Bob says he is again reminded of Erickson's stages of growth and development and that he sensed that a secure attachment enables the parts to be happy and free in that field.

INSIGHTS

Freedom is a field.

As I write this, I'm looking through my windows at two large fields that from the bulk of our family farm. They are green and lush and rife with possibility.

These aren't the fields my parts are running in, but they could be.

This old dairy farm has been in our family for decades. Over the years, we have run freely in it, ridden horses, planted peas and watermelons and grass for cows. It has hosted family softball and volleyball games and our McKnight Family Reunion Olympics.

It is a wide open space, uncluttered, unencumbered, peaceful, serene and secluded—perfect for parts work. It's a safe space makes me think of calm clarity. My dad spends hours upon hours mowing these beloved 40 acres in his red Massey Ferguson tractor. He calls it his meditation, his spiritual practice.

When I was a prison chaplain my closest friend inside was a psych specialist who was also a painter. He introduced me to the work of the Wyeths, and it's often their fields I do pars work in.

"I don't really have studios. I wander around—around people's attics, out in fields, in cellars, anyplace I find that invites me." —Andrew Wyeth

BOB'S NOTES

I named my daughter after my paternal grandma. She embodied love. There was no happier or safer place to be than being with her. She embodied Rumi's "field."

Grandma had a hard life. Born in Pennsylvania in 1916, she was the oldest of 6. At age 9 her father, who was an alcoholic, took off and abandoned the family. Her mother had a "nervous breakdown" and had to be institutionalized. She remained in the institution the rest of her life.

Grandma and her siblings were going to be sent to an orphanage. She knew that the neighbor's wife had tuberculosis and 3 young children. She went to him and asked if she could live with them and help take care of wife and children. He agreed.

Her 5 younger siblings went to his orphanage. Amazingly, they all stayed close the rest of their lives.

The wife of Grandma's neighbor died not long after she came to live with them and she assumed the role of mother and eventually wife. He was 25 years her senior

My grandfather was a hard man who had a hard life as well. In 1900 at age 8 he went to work in the coal mines. He was functionally illiterate. He drank and could be violent. His Parts were just surviving.

How my grandma maintained her loving heart is a miracle.

Often people come in to therapy looking for miracles. They feel like orphans, trapped in the trauma of their past. My grandma reminds me that there is always hope. That inside all of us there is the ability to love and heal. Miracles are real.

SESSION THIRTY-ONE

"By declaring that man is responsible and must actualize the potential meaning of his life, I wish to stress that the true meaning of life is to be discovered in the world rather than within man or his own psyche, as though it were a closed system. I have termed this constitutive characteristic 'the self-transcendence of human existence.' It denotes the fact that being human always points, and is directed, to something or someone, other than oneself—be it a meaning to fulfill or another human being to encounter. The more one forgets himself—by giving himself to a cause to serve or another person to love--the more human he is and the more he actualizes himself. What is called self-actualization is not an attainable aim at all, for the simple reason that the more one would strive for it, the more he would miss it. In other words, self-actualization is possible only as a side-effect of self-transcendence." — Viktor E. Frankl, *Man's Search for Meaning*

As Bob references his notes from the previous week and asks if there is anything in particular I want to get curious about this week, I tell him I want to go deeper within, do the work and seek within.

He asks about the part of me that wants that.
Before he asked, I hadn't seen it as a part.
I identify the part as my Seeker/Searcher.
Bob asks what the part is searching for and I say meaning.

It's a very Self-like part, which is probably part of the reason why I didn't recognize it as a part at first. It's a part that has grown and changed and evolved with me over the years, maturing with me and being a vital part of my life at every stage.

This is the part that wants to go deeper, to suss out meaning, find purpose, identify insight, and get the most out of life.

This is the part that believes the second time you watch a movie or read a book or hear a song is the first. It's this part that studies and analyzes everything—life, love, beliefs, meaning, existence, death, religion, psychology, books, film, and music—over and over again, attempting to get the most out of it as possible.

There's a direct connection between this part and what I do, what I actually practice. I don't just study literature, story, myth, music, religion, psychology, basketball, I practice them. Nearly everything I consume, I consume as a creative, as a creator. Life, my life and everything within it, including that which I consume, study, analyze, is the raw material for my art. And this Seeker/Searcher Part is looking, examining, exploring, seeking, searching everything for meaning—both for itself and for my work.

Bob observes that I'm not just seeking or searching for but actually experiencing meaning, becoming that which I am experiencing.

Another part of me speaks up and warns me against being so concerned with going deeper and seeking meaning and searching that I miss the initial, pure experiences itself, to make sure my Seeker/Searcher Part doesn't put the distance and disconnect of the observer between me and the experiences.

An image of someone at a concert, recording and watching it through their phone instead of taking it in directly comes to mind.

Another part says that's a good reminder, but it's true that I get more out of seeking and studying meaning than not doing it, that I learn more by teaching, experiencing more by sharing. Speaking of sharing, Bob tells he was moved by a recent talk I gave at the Unitarian Universalist Fellowship where he attends and that one of my songs I played afterwards had been his ear worm lately, and my Seeker/Searcher Part and my Sharer/Connector Part find this deeply meaningful.

BOB'S NOTES

My paternal uncle passed away last October. He was 88. I took my parents to the funeral in their small Ohio hometown. The place I most wanted to visit was my Grandma Kuchta's house.

There was a woman standing on the front porch as we were driving by. She waved and I decided to stop the car. Dad and I got out and went to talk to her. She was initially guarded but as Dad shared stories about the growing up and the house, she warmed up and invited us to come in.

The last time I was in that house was over 20 years ago, but it felt like yesterday. Even as I write this now tears come to my eyes.

It's a sacred place. It holds meaning and memories and emotions that go beyond something I can describe with words. I don't even want to try. I just want to be with them.

SESSION THIRTY-TWO

"This is the best day of my life!"

One of my granddaughters said this twice within the last week. On two different occasions, two different days, and she meant it both times.

Like me, she feels things very deeply.

She said it last night when I took her to the circus, which she absolutely loved. She also said it when, because her dad is military and stationed several hours away, I took her to the Daddy-Daughter Dance last week, while dancing with one of her little friends.

I can relate. Today is the best day of my life. As was yesterday. And the day before. And the day before that.

She, along with my other grandchildren and children, family and friends, make every day the best day of my life. Every. Single. Day.

But for this particular granddaughter, who is still young and immature and learning emotional regulation, she not only has many best days of her life, but also many she feels like are the worst.

Following our best day ever at the circus, I had a night of bad dreams and night sweats that kept waking me up, and today, meeting with Bob, I still feel fatigued—which, of course, doesn't change the fact that it, like all the others, is the best day of my life.

When I get curious and do a body scan, I identify a Critic Part in my head, behind my eyes, that looks out with criticism. He's a young business man type, in a dress shirt and tie, and says he's only trying to make me better and help me become a better and better person.

He goes onto to say that he feels mostly unheard, his voice drowned out by all my positive, happy, Best Day Ever Parts.

He says he sees me as too positive, that I'm naïve and a little Pollyannaish.

I share with Bob how it's interesting that this Critic Part is behind my eyes, judging and critiquing because I was called up onto the stage to perform in a skit at the circus last night, something that made my granddaughter ecstatic, which is why did it, but as I watched the video this part pointed out the fact that I had put on a few pounds and need to lose them ASAP.

I had a similar experience recently while listening to a live performance I had given of some of my new songs—listening back I heard all the mistakes and ways I could've played and sung the songs better.

This Critic Part speaks up and says that I need him, need his voice to help me improve and grow and evolve.

Bob has me show this part who I am now.

When this part sees me as I am now, his perspective completely changes.

As part of his transformation and unburdening, he takes of his tie and unbuttons his shirt. Dropping his clipboard on his desk, he leaves his office and walks out into the warmth and glow of the afternoon sun, feeling free and happy.

When I ask him about his job, he says he'd like to continue to make suggestions and offer perspectives, but not overly harsh judgements and criticisms.

INSIGHTS

I spend more extended time with my grandchildren than anyone else except my partner.

And the days I have them are the very best days!

We pretend and play with passionate abandon. We create art and make music. We make our own worlds.

We have more fun and find and create more joy than the human heart can contain.

Recently, one of my granddaughters told her mother that her best friends were me and my other granddaughter.

In middle age I play as much as I did as a kid—maybe more.

And I wouldn't trade it for the whole wide world entire.

I am experiencing and learning what Jesus meant when he said, "unless you change and become like little children, you will never enter the kingdom of heaven. Therefore, whoever humbles himself like a child is the greatest in the kingdom of heaven. And whoever welcomes a little child like this in my name welcomes me."

Parts work is a type of child's play, using all of who we are, imagining and pretending and experiencing the kingdom within us.

BOB'S NOTES

Ho'oponopono is a traditional Hawaiian prayer. It goes as follows:

I'm sorry
Please forgive me
Thank you
I love you

I repeat this probably 5 to 10 times out loud each morning as I prepare to start my day. Usually I have one hand on my heart and the other on my belly.

This is a message to my Parts....from both Parts and from Self. It is about forgiveness and healing relationships.

Whether you call it the "Critic", the "Judge", the "Motivator" or the "Guide"; this is often the Part whose energy creates separation in our system. Separation can trigger fear, abandonment and pain in our Parts. Especially our younger Parts or Exiles.

Making amends is a fundamental part of 12 Step programs such as Alcoholics Anonymous. It encompasses Steps 4-10, going from making a "searching and fearless moral inventory", to asking for healing, to naming how we've harmed other, to making amends when appropriate.

Step 10 states, "Continued to practice these principles in all our affairs" and Step 11 advises to seek "through prayer and meditation to improve our conscious contact with God as we understood him".

Ho-ponopono succinctly guides me through this process of reconciliation.

From the inside, **towards** the inside.
I'm sorry
Please forgive me
Thank you
I love you

SESSION THIRTY-THREE

"What was your original face before your birth?"
"My face? Before I was born?"
"What did it look like?"
"How can I—Wait. I can almost see it. You're asking who I am right? Who I was originally."
"What we call *I* is just a swinging door which moves when we inhale and when we exhale."
"I often ask who I am and why am I here?"
"Who are you and why are you here?"
"I'm searching for my identity and purpose."
"I already told you your identity—what you call I is just a swinging door which moves when we inhale and when we exhale. The soul is here for its own joy. And your purpose . . . well, we do not exist for the sake of something else. We exist for the sake of ourselves. Treat every moment as your last—not preparation for something else."
"Treat every moment as my last."
"And as your first—in the beginner's mind there are many possibilities, but in the expert's there are few"

This weekend I'm giving an inspirational talk on the original self, and I tell Bob that as part of my preparation for that I'd like to do parts work related to it.

I share with Bob how my concept of transformation for each of us is transitioning back as closely as we can to our original selves. This is pure. This is authentic. This is original.

This is who we really are, who we're meant to be—before all of the influences of family and culture and religion and education—all the indoctrination, especially that which happened long before we knew what was going on.

This seems to resonate with Bob and he said that in the framework of IFS activated parts can obscure the Self.

When we get curious I become aware of a Little Boy Part. He is pure joy and innocence and light and excitement and love.

He has a lack of awareness of that which was outside of himself, especially the greater outside world. He doesn't care what other people think of him. He is Self directed.

Bob reminds me to slow down and I realize my mind is rushing, running, racing. I'm out of balance—too much in my head. My intellectual/thinker/reasoner side is more active than my stoical experiential side.

Two Parental Parts show up.

Bob asks if I can ask them if they are willing to stand aside for now so I can interact with the Little Boy Part.

They do.

Another part speaks up and says that my yin and yang are out of balance, that the dance between the two is out of rhythm.

Bob says let's thank that part for that information and ask if it will also step aside and allow us space to interact with the Little Boy Part.

When the other parts have stepped back, there's an exchange between Self and the Little Boy Part.

There's a wonderful, warm energy, pure and joyous, that flows between Self and the Little Boy.

As my other parts witness this they are suddenly in long, ancient robes, as if great thinkers, philosophers, and stoics.

An image of Jesus as a young boy in the temple with older scholars fills the cylindrical canvas of my mind like a cyclorama.

The glow from the energy being exchanged between Self and the Little Boy spills out and onto the other parts, energizing and transforming them.

I'm grateful for my pure and playful childlike nature, the Little Boy Part at the center of me.

Bob and I talk about how much I play. I play with my grandchildren—a lot. I play basketball. I play music. Writing novels is a form of play.

We talk about how transformation and transition are big themes for me, and how I see this process and practice as a return to my original self—an activity that happens best and most when my parts aren't activated and involved, especially my Thinker/Figure-Outer Part.

My Little Boy Part is closer to and on the way toward my Original Self, but not the destination. At six or seven, he, too, has already experienced so much dogma and indoctrination. He's a step closer to home but not home it Self.

BOB'S NOTES

Songs can give us hope. They remind us of things we've forgotten and give us direction.

David Wilcox is a modern folk singer whose songs speak to my soul. One song in particular has been a life raft. It's called "That's What the Lonely is For." It acknowledges that even Lonely has a place and purpose. It motivates us to keep growing and keep following (or creating) the Path.

We all have Parts that have been Exiled. They have experienced trauma. They feel afraid and alone. Protectors try to take care of them, but they always fall short. They are not the solution, but they also need to be honored.

As we honor the Parts they un-blend. As they un-blend, the light of Self shines upon the Path.

Working with Parts is something we experience. Something we do. It is an active process. Another David Wilcox song, "We Make the Way by Walking," embodies this.

I am walking the IFS path, and hoping to support others while they walk it as well.

The Way unfolds.

SESSION THIRTY-FOUR

A large yellow tractor, stabilizer legs extended, backhoe plunging down into the earth, scooping up bucket fulls of dirt and robotically rotating the boom to dump them in rising piles to the side.

The smell of damp dirt and wet clay.

A growing hole like an open grave in the earth behind the auditorium of the old redbrick elementary school.

The tractor operator balances his grandson on his lap, and they both wave to his wife, who steps out of portable classroom behind them.

Suddenly, I'm standing in a small crowd of townspeople gathered in expectation.

A woman who died in a car accident during the Christmas holidays turns toward me and asks how my life is going, and remarks that it's significant that the tractor is digging since lately I've been talking about and teaching on digging down to our original selves.

I recall being near this same spot as a little boy with my father and jumping into a recently dug hole and cutting the side of my foot on a piece of glass hidden in the dirt.

I share this dream and memory with Bob and wonder at what it might mean.

He asks if we can have my Figure-Outer/Analyzer Part step back.

There's some resistance as the part is hesitant to do so.

My Figure-Outer/Analyzer Part, which resides in my head, says it is vital for it to find the message—and not just in this dream, but in life itself.

I think about how much this is a Self-like part. I spend much of my time exploring and analyzing—everything from life itself, to meaning, to purpose, to death, to religion, to psychology, to literature, film, music, often enjoying the analysis of a work of art nearly as much as the art itself.

Bob asks again if the Analytical Part will step back—and eventually he does.

He joins me beside the lake at our family farm, where we experience stillness and calm and—then there's a shift from my head to my heart to my lower abdomen—and in there I see how when my Analytical Part is over active it can cause distance to open up between me and direct experience.

Moving forward with greater awareness and less over-activity by my Analytical Part, I hope for more stillness and calm and curiosity and direct experience, saving analysis for later in the process if needed.

Once again I am seeing that in the balance between intellect and intuition I'm erring on the side of the intellectual and analytical.

Far too often even when I am still in every other way, my mind is not.

"Be still and know" comes to mind.

When I share this with Bob, he reminds me that it's "be still and know," not "be still and figure out."

INSIGHTS

Rediscovering and returning to our original Self is one of our most important and significant tasks, an ongoing process that is the work of a lifetime.

In IFS, the Self refers to our core nature, our essence, our seat of consciousness, who we truly are, and it is present and constant regardless of the situation. It is something we're born with and have access to, rather than something that we create.

Long before we have the awareness to even know what's happening, let alone the ability to do anything about it, we are indoctrinated, told what to think and believe, given paradigms with which to interpret the world, others, and ourselves. Parents, peers, culture, religion, politics, education, and trillion other things put us through an intense process of inculcation and propagandism.

Layer upon layer of the dirt and detritus of life cover and bury and hide and obscure our original, essential Self.

Burdened parts become dark clouds that blot out the sun of Self. They don't change or alter the sun, but they do obscure and diffuse it.

Our work is as the archeologists of our own souls. We, with shovels and picks and brooms and brushes, excavate the original, sacred Self buried beneath the burdens of beliefs like the sands of time.

BOB'S NOTES

At the beginning of this session Michael described experiencing the "smell of damp dirt and wet clay." In that moment he was very present.

The sense of smell is particularly linked to memories and emotions. It can also be used to bring our Parts into the present moment using scents such as mint or citrus.

My EMDR trainer, Roy Kiesling, encouraged us to use the senses to help ground people. Part of preparing people for EMDR is helping them access safety and containment. This is done using imagery as well as bilateral stimulation when appropriate.

The "Place" exercise involves helping the client identify a place that has been secure and comforting to them. The clinician guides the client to become present in that space by tuning in to each of their senses; gradually exposing them to their memories of what the place looks like, sounds like, smells like and feels like (tactilely).

This is followed by helping them embody the experience, encouraging them to notice how their entire system is responding to being in that place. Using IFS, we might ask them to get curious about how their Parts are responding.

The "Place" imagery can also be used to nurture secure attachment between Parts and Self. One of my clients has created a treehouse where her younger Parts are able to play and feel safe. The trunk of the tree and roots represent Self. In the field where the tree is, there are small houses where different Protectors reside. She also has what she calls a "safe house" where she will take Parts when they feel overwhelmed and need a 1:1 connection. When a number of Parts are blended we ask them to join her and sit in a circle with Self (the base of tree) serving as the grounding point.

She returns to this "Place" at some point at least every other session. It is the experiential map that brings her back to safety, security and Self. It is her home.

SESSION THIRTY-FIVE

Deadline looming.
    Friday afternoon.
    End of the workweek just hours away.
    So much to do. So little time left.
    Head down, nose to the grindstone.
    In my session with Bob today, he asks me to go somewhere and have my parts sit around me.
    We sit on stones under a tree next to the lake on the Old Dairy Farm, which our family owns.
    As I scan the circle, from right to left, I see my parts sitting with me—until I get to the bottom of the circle. Then from that point on the entire left side is blurry and no parts are present.
    When I search for them, I find them in an upscale space that's a combination of bank building and lawyers office with leather couches and chairs, large cherry-wood desks and bookshelves.
    The Busy Working Parts have their heads down, working on paperwork piled high on their desks. They are very focused on their jobs, which is primarily of keeping track of things, and

they are intrinsically motivated and don't have a direct boss or supervisor.

They say they are far too busy to join us at the lake.

I walk in and tell them that the work can wait and that we're closing the offices so they can join us at the farm, and though they don't particularly want to, they realize that I'm the boss, which means it's okay.

When we reach the farm, they really don't want to sit in a circle on stones, so they kayak and swim and play volleyball, enjoying themselves and relaxing while expending energy.

Bob asks if these are legacy parts and I know immediately that they are. They are doing jobs that were given to them by the generation before them and those were given to them by the generation before them.

Bob asks if this is related to what's happening with my dad (he just had open-heart surgery) and my family responsibilities.

And I realize that it is. Not only had I attended a family company meeting recently and spoke to him about it, but during his recovery in the hospital we had spent a lot of time hearing him and his brother tell family stories and share memories.

This experience, which relates to things happening both inside of me and outside in our family, is related to family responsibility and generational legacy, and I find it instructive and interesting the these parts went from the family business to the family farm.

BOB'S NOTES

One of my clients is a dynamic young woman navigating motherhood, a new relationship, and furthering her education. Underlying this are family of origin experiences that have nurtured her Exiles and molded her Protectors.

In a recent session we were getting curious about being a mom and being a daughter. One Part told her to "get a hold or her life" while another asked (or exclaimed), "What is wrong with you!"

As we sat with these Part's another powerful voice spoke out to remind her, "I bring the war...I am the war...I'm gonna cause chaos...I am evil!"

Viscerally she felt her mother's presence inside of her. She recalled memories of her maternal grandmother and stories about how her mother was raised.

Her daughter is two years old. She tearfully acknowledged times she has found that voice directed at her daughter's behavior.

This was a Legacy. Part or Parts carrying something she did not create, but is none the less attached to her now.

We all carry them in one way or another.

Take a moment to slow down.

Let yourself breath.

Invite curiosity as you connect with memories of your family and stories of your ancestors.

There is nothing you need to do or change or fix right now.

Just observe.

If you'd like to, jot down a few things you noticed.

SESSION THIRTY-SIX

"Don't forget that manuscript is due to your editor in two weeks. Better figure out what your word count for each day needs to be and make sure you're hitting it."

"I got this. I'm in good shape."

"Glad you think so, but don't forget you also need to be prepping for your upcoming conference and songwriters event."

"I am."

"Okay, but there's a lot of moving parts to manage and coordinate. Are you sure you haven't forgotten anything?"

"No. Not positive."

"You better go through them again and double check. And you should make a list so you don't forget anything. And with all this going on don't forget you need to be reading and meditating more and you want to get back to doing yoga."

In my session with Bob today I begin by talking about all the great things happening, including my dad's recovery from open-heart surgery, how good my family and friends are doing, and how well my writing and music are going.

When we discuss some of my upcoming events and opportunities I become aware of an activated part.

Getting curious, I see a Reminder Part, who believes his job is to remind me of all I need to be doing—writing more, meditating more, reading more, spending even more time with family, and prepping for my upcoming conferences, book releases, and songwriter events. This part is concerned that I'm spending so much time caring for my dad and grandchildren that I'm not doing enough in other areas.

This Reminder Part is around thirty, but seems older, and sees me as late teens or early twenties. Very much a Parental-type Part, he's constantly reminding me of what else I need to be doing, and can be pushy and relentless in this role.

My Younger Parts are both grateful for the reminders and resent them, appreciating the concern, but resisting the relentless nature of it and preferring to do things on their own schedule and at their own pace.

My Reminder Part speaks directly to my Overly Responsible Part, pushing him to take even more responsibility and to do more.

My Overly Responsible Part wants to be the the one who helps and meets the needs of my loved ones, especially my children and grandchildren, and this Reminder Part continuously feeds his sense of responsibility.

Showing the Reminder Part who I am, he sees that I always get everything done and I don't need incessant reminders. Through this process of increased awareness, he agrees to recalibrate his perception and take a different approach to his job. He now sees occasional reminders are helpful, but constant, incessant ones are not only not necessary, but can interrupt flow and decrease serenity.

BOB'S NOTES

Where are your Parts focusing? Are they looking back to the past, ahead to the future, or seeing what is present.

Some of my Parts are time travelers. They can even be like Benedict Cumberbatch's character, Dr. Strange, from Marvel's Avengers and exist in "multiverses." They can seek the infinite possibilities of what "might be" or "could have been" for solutions, reminders or regrets.

They can become exhausted.

Allow yourself to get curious about any Parts present within you that might be exhausted or overwhelmed.

Invite them to follow your breath.

In and out...
In and out...
In and out...

Place your hand/s wherever they might be present in or around your body.

In and out...
In and out...
In and out...

Ask them who they think you are.

In and out...
In and out...
In and out...
Invite them to become aware of you as you are now
In and out...
In and out...
In and out...
Acknowledge how they are feeling
In and out...
In and out...
In and out...
Extend gratitude and appreciation.
I'm sorry.
Please forgive me.
Thank you.
I love you.

SESSION THIRTY-SEVEN

An Ohio-class nuclear-powered submarine, silently cruising at 20 knots, displacing 18,750 tons of water in the world's largest ocean.

Earlier in the day, it left Pearl Harbor in Hawaii, slipping beneath the waves, cocooning its passengers in one of the world's most technologically advanced pieces of equipment as they dive dark depths on extended strategic deterrent patrols.

Deep inside this modern marvel of imagination and engineering a highly trained and skilled technician studies gauges and screens, closely monitoring the operation of this complex and sophisticated system.

When I get curious in my session with Bob today, I identify a Monitor Part, who believes his job is to keep things running at an optimal level.

He monitors my systems closely in an attempt to identify potential issues before they become problems. His approach to his job leads him to endeavor to prevent or at least mitigate bad things from happening before they do. He reads the monitors and interprets the data from the sensors, aiming to avoid anything that causes issues or threatens tranquility or prevents pleasure.

Like many of my parts he takes an overly responsible approach to his job, doing far more than he should and feeling more responsible than he is.

He sees me as a little boy in need of protecting and this is his way of doing that.

When Bob asks me to let him see me as I am now I find him in the engine room of an Ohio-class nuclear submarine carefully monitoring the systems.

When I walk across the metal catwalk grate to him, he turns and says, "I'm doing this all for you."

We spend time together and he soon sees he has no need to do what he's been doing, especially the way he's been doing it.

There's an exchange of energy, a flow from Self to him that leads to a newfound freedom.

Gradually, he feels free from the weight of the responsibility he's been carrying, relieved to not have to be responsible for all the systems of all the other parts.

Eventually, he says he'd like to continue his job of monitoring and notifying, but staying out of the way of other parts, allowing them to deal with their jobs and the issues involved with them in their own way.

He sees how what he's been doing, in taking responsibility for other parts, in trying to prevent or fix any problems, he's getting in their way, creating a barrier to direct experience, robbing them of opportunities for growth.

INSIGHTS

Not surprisingly, Internal Family Systems is all about, among many other things, systems.

A system is a group of interacting or interrelated elements or parts of an interconnecting network that act according to a set of rules to form a unified whole in order to perform a particular function or for a particular purpose.

I am made up of systems. My systems have systems.

I am my systems, as you are yours.

We are largely unaware of our systems.

Through IFS we explore our systems and the parts that form them. We identify and interact with parts that are activated, blended, and burdened in such a way as to have an (often unhealthy or undesired) impact on the system they are an interconnected part of.

I find it fascinating that I have a part that monitors my systems.

It makes a certain sense, of course, but I find it interesting and instructive that without the IFS model and the accompanying parts work I could've gone my entire life without ever becoming aware of this part.

Because of IFS I am not only aware of the part but get to explore his role and beliefs, both as an individual part and a part of the whole.

BOB'S NOTES

In 1985, a 10 hour PBS series titled "Bradshaw On: The Family" was aired. It introduced family systems theory to the mainstream population and became a vital part of the "self help" movement.

The creator, John Bradshaw, had left the seminary in his early years to teach. A recovering addict himself, he became a psychologist whose series and subsequent books spoke from the heart. They provided a theoretical foundation that helped people make sense of their experiences.

His second PBS show was entitled "Healing the Shame that Binds You" which was followed by "Homecoming: Reclaiming and Championing your Inner Child."

When I was introduced to IFS, I was taken back to my exposure to John Bradshaw. IFS translates what he taught us to our inner world. It shows us there is a parallel between our outer and inner experiences. Ultimately, things make sense when we are able to approach them with curiosity.

Within and **without**, Bradshaw and IFS give our "monitor" Parts clear maps to follow.

SESSION THIRTY-EIGHT

"I were little happy if I could say how much!"

This line from Shakespeare's "Much ado about Nothing" so often describes how I feel. The entire quote is "Silence is the perfect herald of joy. I were little happy if I could say how much." And though I often break that sacred silence and attempt to say and sing and describe and write how much, I can never adequately express my gratitude and joy.

As happy weeks go, this one is up in the stratosphere among the very highest. My family is gaining two new members—one by birth and one by marriage—and we will have wonderful and fitting celebrations for both. And I were little happy if I could say how much.

I am beyond excited, beyond thrilled, beyond grateful.

I am happy and peaceful, calm and thankful.

And yet...

This morning I woke up with a tightness around my heart.

It is so out of nowhere and in such contrast to everything else I'm feeling that I wonder if it's subconscious, some sort of residual remnants from my dreams.

Bob suggests we get curious.

As we do, no activated parts emerge.

It's the first time this has happened.

I stay still and quiet and present, continuing to be curious.

Eventually, a part that is not mine, an invisible legacy part gripping my heart, manifests. The message this part has is that I'm too calm, not worried enough, not stressed enough about the monumental events happening in my life and the life of my family.

Bob says it sounds like an unattached burden to him.

This means that the part did not originate with me. Its story and beliefs are not mine. It came from outside of me, passed down like a legacy.

It doesn't trust my calm, my peace, my security, so it pushes me to be nervous and anxious.

It's grip around my heart is loosening now that it has lost its cloak of invisibility.

Bob asks if I'm sure it's not mine, not a part of me.

I tell him I am sure that it's not.

He suggests that I release its energy to some element outside of me—earth, wind, fire or water.

I feel as though it needs to be released not just to air, but to wind to match its energy.

Bob leads me through the process and I open myself up and release this unwanted energy to the wind. It flies out of me as I blow out and tell it that it is against my nature and unwanted here.

Once it is gone, cast out into the wind, I fill that space it has been occupying with a calm, peaceful, warm glow.

Bob says he feels like this is related to something generational.

I agree.

I feel completely free of it, unburdened, unblended, left only with the joy that defies description, and in the full face of which words fail.

INSIGHTS

Lay it down.

Let it go.

Experience sweet release.

Legacy or not, letting go of burdens, laying them down, giving them up—to air, fire, earth, or water brings true freedom.

There are a variety of ways to lay down your burdens.

You can "Cast your cares on the Lord for he cares for you."

You can take a few steps—especially these first three: We admitted we were powerless over our burdens—that our lives had become unmanageable. Came to believe that a Power greater than ourselves could restore us to sanity. Made a decision to turn our will and our lives over to the care of God as we understood Him.

You can say a prayer: God grant me the serenity to accept the things I cannot change; courage to change the things I can; and wisdom to know the difference.

Of course, it's not just in the saying of the above words, but in the practice of them that we find true release.

I attempt to both say and practice the above—and to add to

them IFS parts work, which is the experiential practice and process of unburdening.

Unblended and unburdened parts, and the pure Self energy that flows to and through them leads to a truly serene freedom.

BOB'S NOTES

About 15 years ago I attended a daylong training by Dr. Peter Levine. He is the developer of Somatic Experiencing, a body based (bottom up) approach to heal trauma.

He began the training by having us watch two nature videos designed to illustrate how the body responds to trauma.

The first showed a gazelle being chased by a cheetah. When it was slowed down you see that the gazelle collapses to the ground never being touched by the cheetah. The chase illustrated the "mammalian" brain trying to survive by either fleeing (to live) or fighting (to feed). When the gazelle's body recognized it wasn't going to escape (and the gazelle knew fighting was not an option), it systems shut down in collapse, regressing to the survival method of the more primitive "reptilian" part of the brain.

He likened this to what IFS might call the Firefighter of shutting down, or dissociation. We too regress back down the evolutionary path to more "primitive" methods of survival when our lives, or our Parts, are compromised.

However, it was the second video that held the key. It

showed what animals can teach us about how to release and heal trauma. In it you see a polar bear that is running on the ice suddenly collapse. It has been shot with a tranquilizer dart and tagged so it can be tracked. This is only the prelude.

After a time lapsed period on the video, you see the polar bear as it begins to come to. It is still lying down, but its legs and body begin to tremble. After a period of time shaking, the polar bear stands and goes on its way.

The polar bear does not have PTSD. Its trauma is released instead of carried.

Its body naturally reenacted the flight process. In doing so it released the energy that you and I so often suppress and try to control...which then becomes the trauma we carry. Our Manager Protectors dedicate themselves to preventing it from ever happening again . . . but in the process they often recreate its experience

So this brings us back to the body. The body knows. As Dutch psychiatrist Bessel van der Kolk put it, "The Body Keeps the Score."

But what can we do about it?

For the polar bear, the voice came out with physiological trembling and release. It was unburdened. Just like that.

For Michael the Parts often resided within his body as well. Throughout this book he has shared his experiences of listening to their voices of. They came out in stories, tears, images, emotions and movement. They were experienced. They were witnessed. They were alive. Many of them were unburdened.

A few months ago I met with a healer who encouraged me to spend time each day allowing my body physically release. Each morning before I start my day I take time to connect to my body's energy and let it release. Whatever Parts are present "speak" as they see fit.

Afterwards, while I may not be as free as the polar bear, and I find I am more connected to Self energy. Unwound. Released. Unblended. In the process of unburdening.

We innately have the capacity to release and heal.

MY FIRST YEAR WITH IFS

My first year with IFS was remarkable. And it was just the beginning.

It has been a journey within a journey, enabling me to continue the spiritual expedition I have been on while also taking rewarding, sometimes unexpected excursions—all with a wise guide alongside.

Thank you for taking this journey with us.

In many ways, my IFS work with Bob has been a continuation and a deepening of work I've been doing for most of my life. In other ways, it has been refreshingly new.

IFS has given me new and sharper tools for my work of building a life, crafting a soul, hewing a self, while also providing me with an experienced craftsman to gently teach me how to better use them.

It has also provided me with a new paradigm, a new prism to see through—and a new vocabulary to express what I see.

The practice of IFS is the most complete form of therapy I've ever encountered. It honors my complexity and sophistication, my rich internal tapestry, my mosaic mind, the multiverse within me.

Its insistence that there are no bad parts resonates with me, its view of the self as complete aligns with my experience, and the self-led nature of its practice fits as if tailored specifically for me. And unlike other conceptualizations and approaches, the application of IFS taps into the totality of my being—mind and body, spirit and soul, self and parts. It's intellectual and intuitive, mental and emotional, and ultimately imaginatively experiential.

The practice of self-led therapy, particularly with such a gifted, wise, and compassionate therapist, has given me many gifts, but none more impactful than increased clarity and freedom. The experience of unblending has given me much greater clarity and the process of unburdening has exponentially increased my freedom.

My experience of IFS, this practice of self-led leadership, has led to a greater, more consistent self-led life. Rather than being ruled, even briefly, by unruly, activated parts, blended with each other and burdened by errant beliefs, I live a life even more self-directed, more centered in Self. Not self-centered, which has a negative connotation, but centered in and by the Self.

Activated, blended, and burdened parts create barriers to self-flow, cells that imprison and obscure my true Self. My practice of IFS calms these parts, unblends and unburdens them, leading to a return to my original self and the freedom needed to live from that sacred place.

I love and appreciate my parts and the jobs they do. It's as if my Self is their wise, calm, compassionate old parent and they his well-meaning but sometime immature, impulsive, radicalized children, giving it their all, doing their best, but in need of nurture and guidance. Practicing IFS is the process by which this happens in me.

The more my parts are unblended and unburdened, the more my Self is leading, the more I experience calm, compassion, clarity, creativity, connectedness, courage, confidence, and curiosity, the more I am present, patient, persistent, playful, and have perspective.

My first year with IFS was both a culmination of the work I had done previously, all the paths I traveled before, and a new beginning—a way being that I will explore and practice for the rest of my life.

My sincere hope is that in sharing aspects of my journey with you, you will be inspired and moved and gain greater clarity and insight for your own journey, that you will curiously embrace with compassion all of who you are, and that you will have the courage and confidence in your own process of freeing your Self, liberating your soul and living your very best self-led life.

BOB'S NOTES

I have dealt with chronic lower back pain since I was a teenager. I injured myself while pitching for the 11-12 year old Little League team representing my hometown in the regional All Star games.

The field we played on in Big Bear didn't have a pitcher's mound, so I was used to pitching from a flat surface. During the All Star games we played in another town where the field had the normal pitcher's mound.

Biomechanically, my body was used to completing the task of pitching on flat ground. It experienced most of the physiological trauma twice that All Star week while throwing 50 to 60 pitches off a mound. It anticipated a certain outcome but experienced another. Over and over again.

I have learned a few things living in my body and managing lower back pain over the past 39 years.
 1. Good lumbar support is a necessity
 2. The more flexible I am (stretching) the better
 3. I need a firm bed for rest/sleep
 4. Therapy (massage and chiropractic) help me stay aligned.
 5. The older I get the slower I need to go

6. Release the pain

These lessons managing the physical consequences of that trauma serve me well in the other areas of my life (when I remember and choose to follow them). IFS is the map that reminds me of the way.

It is a process.
Make sure you have good support and a secure foundation.
Be flexible and willing to ask for help.
Take it easy.
Breathe.
Let go.

I appreciate Michael inviting me to be a part of this book. As long as I can remember I've wanted to be a writer. I have enjoyed writing these brief reflections and hope you find them helpful.

Thank you for spending time with us.

CONTACT

To book Michael Lister for a consulting or life coaching session or to have him give an inspirational or motivational talk to your organization you may contact him through his website: www.MichaelLister.com

Bob Kuchta can be reached through his email address Bobkuchtacounseling@Gmail.com

ABOUT THE AUTHOR

Michael Lister is a *New York Times* bestselling and award-winning novelist, renowned for his acclaimed John Jordan "Blood" mystery thriller series, his Burke and Blade PI "Night" series, his Jimmy Riley 40s noir "Big" series, and his standalone thrillers, *Double Exposure* and *Burnt Offerings*.

A native Floridian, Michael grew up in the small town of Wewahitchka near the Gulf of Mexico and the Apalachicola River and celebrated for its tupelo honey.

With a lifelong passion for storytelling, Michael's love for language and narrative is deeply rooted in the Southern tradition. Before becoming a full-time novelist in 2000, he had a diverse career that included teaching high school, working as a college professor, and inspirational speaker. He also owned and operated a bookstore, wrote a popular syndicated column, served as a newspaper editor, and engaged in community theater as a writer, director, and actor. His extensive experience in creative fields includes lecturing on creative writing, film, literature, spirituality, and self-help.

In the 1990s, Michael served as the youngest chaplain within the Florida Department of Corrections. His decade-long tenure as a chaplain at three facilities in Florida's Panhandle inspired his first novel, *Power in the Blood* (1997), which received critical acclaim.

In addition to the John Jordan series, Michael is the author of the Burke and Blade Panama City Beach PI series (including *The Night Of*), the 1940s Jimmy Riley noir series (starting with

The Big Goodbye), and thrillers such as *Double Exposure, Burnt Offerings,* and *Separation Anxiety.*

Michael's work has earned two Florida Book Awards and landed him on both the *New York Times* and *USA Today* Bestseller lists. His novels have been translated into German and adapted for the stage. *Double Exposure* is currently in development for a feature film, and the John Jordan series is being adapted for television.

Michael is also an exceptional inspirational and motivational speaker whose charisma and dynamic delivery make a lasting impact, and a gifted singer-songwriter, whose music has been praised for its humanity, storytelling, and haunting beauty.

Michael resides in North Florida, where he balances his writing with time spent with family and friends, playing basketball, and making music.

ABOUT THE AUTHOR

Bob Kuchta is a Licensed Clinical Social Worker who has been practicing therapy for 17 years. He had varied roles in the child welfare system in the 11 years leading up to this. He was introduced to IFS nine years ago and has used it as his primary form of therapy for the last four years. Originally from Big Bear California, he currently lives in Panama City, Florida with his wife Mandy, their two children Jimmy and Mary, and an assortment of animals.

ALSO BY MICHAEL LISTER

(Inspirational Self-help Books)

Meaning Every Moment

The Meaning of Life in Movies

Finding the Way Again

More: Do More of What Matters Most and Discover the Life of Your Dreams

My First Year with IFS Therapy

The You You've Been Looking For: Rediscovering and Returning to Your Original Self through Spirituality, Psychology, and Internal Family Systems

(John Jordan Mysteries)

Power in the Blood

Blood of the Lamb

The Body and the Blood

Double Exposure

Blood Sacrifice

Rivers to Blood

Burnt Offerings

Innocent Blood

(Special Introduction by Michael Connelly)

Separation Anxiety

Blood Money

Blood Moon

Thunder Beach

Blood Cries

A Certain Retribution

Blood Oath

Blood Work

Cold Blood

Blood Betrayal

Blood Shot

Blood Ties

Blood Stone

Blood Trail

Bloodshed

Blue Blood

And the Sea Became Blood

The Blood-Dimmed Tide

Blood and Sand

A John Jordan Christmas

Blood Lure

Blood Pathogen

Beneath a Blood-Red Sky

Out for Blood

What Child is This?

Blood Reckoning

A Rush of Blood

(Burke and Blade Mystery Thrillers)

The Night Of

The Night in Question

All Night Long

Dead of Night
Dark of Night
Gone in the Night

(Jimmy Riley Novels)
The Girl Who Said Goodbye
The Girl in the Grave
The Girl at the End of the Long Dark Night
The Girl Who Cried Blood Tears
The Girl Who Blew Up the World

(Merrick McKnight / Reggie Summers Novels)
Thunder Beach
A Certain Retribution
Blood Oath
Blood Shot

(Remington James Novels)
Double Exposure
(includes intro by Michael Connelly)
Separation Anxiety
Blood Shot

(Sam Michaels / Daniel Davis Novels)
Burnt Offerings
Blood Oath
Cold Blood
Blood Shot

(Love Stories)

Carrie's Gift

(Short Story Collections)

North Florida Noir

Florida Heat Wave

Delta Blues

Another Quiet Night in Desperation

Sign up for Michael's newsletter go to www.MichaelLister.com and receive a free book.

www.ingramcontent.com/pod-product-compliance
Lightning Source LLC
Chambersburg PA
CBHW030332230426
43661CB00032B/1380/J